Design & Solidarity

T0285181

Design & Solidarity

Conversations on Collective Futures

Rafi Segal and

Marisa Morán Jahn

With

Mercedes Bidart

Arturo Escobar

Michael Hardt

Greg Lindsay

Jessica Gordon Nembhard

Ai-jen Poo, and

Trebor Scholz

COLUMBIA UNIVERSITY PRESS / NEW YORK

Columbia University Press
Publishers Since 1893
New York   Chichester, West Sussex
cup.columbia.edu

Library of Congress Cataloging-in-Publication Data
Names: Jahn, Marisa, 1977- interviewer. | Segal, Rafi, interviewer.
Title: Design and solidarity : conversations on collective futures /
    Rafi Segal and Marisa Morán Jahn ; with Mercedes Bidart,
    Arturo Escobar, Michael Hardt, Greg Lindsay, Jessica Gordon
    Nembhard, Ai-jen Poo, and Trebor Scholz.
Description: New York : Columbia University Press, [2022] | Includes
    index. | Identifiers: LCCN 2022012907 | ISBN 9780231204040
    (hardback) | ISBN 9780231204057 (trade paperback) |
    ISBN 9780231555340 (ebook)
Subjects: LCSH: Design—Social aspects. | Mutualism.
Classification: LCC NK1520 .J34 2022 | DDC 745.4—dc23/eng/20220629
LC record available at https://lccn.loc.gov/2022012907

Columbia University Press books are printed
    on permanent and durable acid-free paper.

Cover design: Marisa Morán Jahn

Printed and bound by CPI Group (UK) Ltd, Croydon, CR0 4YY

Contents

Introduction: Design Solidarity   1
Marisa Morán Jahn and Rafi Segal

Conversations
On the Common   31
Michael Hardt

On Self-Determination in a World Where Many Worlds Fit   41
Arturo Escobar

On Solidarity and Political Emancipation   57
Jessica Gordon Nembhard

On Labor and Cooperatives   69
Trebor Scholz

On Mutual Aid Societies and Digital-First Organizing   87
Greg Lindsay

On Digital Platforms in Informal Economies   99
Mercedes Bidart

On Mutualism and Care   113
Ai-jen Poo

Essays
Architecture for New Collectives   127
Rafi Segal

Creation as Counterpower   157
Marisa Morán Jahn

Carehaus: Designing for Care   183
Marisa Morán Jahn and Rafi Segal

Acknowledgements   205
About the Authors and Contributors   207
Index   213

Design & Solidarity

Design Solidarity

Marisa Morán Jahn and Rafi Segal

Design (for, with, and as) Solidarity

What does it mean to design spaces for—and of—solidarity? How does solidarity inform design, and how can design enable new forms of solidarity to emerge? Design and solidarity, or perhaps simply *design solidarity*, reflects on these questions and their relevance today.

On a fundamental level, the design of physical space and the spatial relationships it defines can strengthen, weaken, or obviate solidarity. Through their spatial layout, structure, location, the design of physical spaces and their functions reflects the ways in which they contribute to group solidarity. For example, in the United States, town halls have historically been designed to enabled residents to gather together to discuss, debate, and collectively decide on community matters. So, too, a cultural heritage (e.g., musical traditions, textiles, and artifacts) requires a repository for those collective assets which in turn require management and upkeep.

Beyond their utilitarian purpose, buildings and urban forms—as well as the activities they engender—commemorate and concretize historically specific shared beliefs. In the same way that spaces can be designed to segregate, isolate, and enforce supervision for private gain or authoritarian control, they can also be shaped to promote mutualism, self-determination, and democracy (as with community centers, farmers markets, public spaces of assembly, urban squares, and parks). Dolores Hayden chronicles a nineteenth- and

We use the term design *to refer to a field that broadly encompasses art, architecture, and media as well as the design of objects, graphics, urban spaces, services, strategies, experiences, and more. While we are interdisciplinary practitioners whose work bisects many of these fields, in this book we focus on the spatial and public dimensions of design as it draws most heavily from our own respective training and work as an artist and an architect.*

We use the term solidarity *to refer to the act of building alliances within and across communities in order to achieve socioeconomic equity. Solidarity is fundamental to dismantling what J. K. Gibson-Graham refer to as "capitalocentrism."**

We understand mutualism *as referring to a looser set of principles, occurring along different scales from the microeconomic (soup swaps or care swaps) to the macroeconomic (multinational labor agreements). In comparison to mutualism, solidarity carries a stronger level of commitment, intentionality, and political aspiration that does not accept late capitalism as a fait accompli. Solidarity redistributes power.*

We use the word commons *to refer to shared assets, which include, most obviously, land, water, food, and urban space; we also use it to refer to shared imaginaries, stories, iconographies, and histories. In all cases, commons are shared assets that necessarily need to be maintained, a process that itself builds solidarity.*

---

* J. K. Gibson-Graham, *A Postcapitalist Politics* (Minneapolis: Minnesota University Press, 2006), 57.

Centrally located in Manhattan, Union Square Park has functioned as a public gathering place for U.S. social movements since the nineteenth century. Despite this storied history, in 2008, a Business Improvement District with support of then-Mayor Bloomberg sought to convert the park's landmark pavilion into a privately owned, upscale restaurant, only adding to the density of restaurants already in the surrounding neighborhood. Opposition led by grassroots organizers, families, artists, and NYC Park Advocates called out Bloomberg's neoliberal maneuver as an encroachment on the right to publicly assemble, a reduction of usable space, and the privatization of the commons. After a decade of struggle, the pavilion was leased to a restaurant whose menu is unaffordable by the city's majority. Photo by Marisa Morán Jahn, 2022..

early twentieth-century movement to communalize living, care, and cooking through changes to the floor plan of the American family home, in turn transforming the very conception of the nuclear family.[1] This and other examples point out the historical contingencies of mutualism. Echoed perhaps in simpler terms, mutualism is a condition that needs an architectural or urban "body" instantiated at a certain time, place, and size.

At times, preserving public benefits (clean water, unpolluted air, coastal access, sunlight) requires anticipating, rendering, and visualizing what should *not* be designed. This might take the form of building limits or zoning envelopes. Some examples include the preservation of green spaces within and outside the city or the protection of urban streets and parks from overshadowing. In other words, designing for mutual benefit may involve obviating, regulating, or modulating the interests of private parties.

While architecture and urban space promise durability and permanence, their implementation requires long, complex processes and many resources. On the other hand, ephemeral and impermanent interventions in public spaces—pop-ups, temporary performances, processions, and other artistic spatial practices—allow groups to respond to changing political contexts with greater alacrity.

For example, nimble setups and breakdowns for gatherings in an urban space provide dexterity. Here, the ability to quickly negotiate visibility can prove critical for those from historically underrepresented groups. In the recent movement to replace the United States' 1,400+ monuments memorializing white supremacist and genocidal leaders, artists played a key role by quickly creating "lightweight" and temporary public interventions envisioning historical alternatives. In 2017, Glenn Cantave and the collective he founded, Movers and Shakers, created site-specific alternative monuments featuring women, people of color, and LGBTQIA2S+ icons.[1] Accessed via augmented reality, the images and renderings were cost-efficient to generate and enabled the group to incite the participation of diverse publics. In this example, the quick response time met the collective's goal to jump-start redesigning public spaces.

Furthermore, such strategies are often financially and politically more accessible for marginalized communities and/or precarious groups (precariats), as they do not require the intensive resources and capital, established networks, and managerial systems that architecture demands. Through artistic spatial practices, emerging or historically marginalized communities can assert their civic value and set into motion longer-term material transformations, socioeconomic equity, and/or political influence.

In the United States, the cultural erasure and legal exclusion of domestic workers reached an inflection point in 2010 when immigrant women of color in New York led a decade-long campaign demanding the same rights as other workers. The initial legislation granted New York state's two hundred thousand nannies, housekeepers, and caregivers overtime wage, meal breaks, and paved the path for even more comprehensive laws that have till now passed in ten other states and two cities.

After the initial victory, members of the National Domestic Workers Alliance (NDWA) reached out to Marisa Morán Jahn to create new ways to help communicate the new laws and more broadly help shift how our nation values care. Among other artworks and tools cocreated with domestic workers, Jahn designed a mobile studio called the NannyVan, a bright orange, souped-up 1976 Chevy van replete with roll-out craft carts and benches that created temporary collective spaces at playgrounds, markets, and toddler story time hour at public libraries. Through the Nannyvan and a second mobile studio, the CareForce One, Jahn's team[2] convened domestic workers and domestic employers to exchange personal stories, resources such as know your rights tips, and information about the growing movement. The aim was to invite participants in these pop-up spaces to begin self-identifying as domestic workers and recognize their experiences within broader historical narratives and structural injustices. As this example shows, design solidarity includes not only the creation of things but also the narratives they engender and the values they historicize.

Daniel Rodriguez, the first DREAMer[3] to graduate from law school in the United States and the son of a domestic worker, conveyed the NannyVan's superpowers of adroitness and access: "When I think about the NannyVan, I think about mobility," he said. "It's really important for projects like the NannyVan to go into communities and use that mobility to go where other individuals and organizations can't go."[4] Similar words were echoed by officers of the U.S. Department of Labor who acknowledged their limitations and challenges reaching informal workers given their focus on salaried workers. Indeed, conversations between Jahn and NDWA further revealed the NannyVan and CareForce One's strength in claiming public space for domestic workers and shifting public awareness around their essential yet invisibilized labor. Jahn shares segments of her journey later in this book (see essay entitled "Creation as Counterpower").

While Jahn's essay focuses on the power of identify and our roles within the spectrum of care, "Carehaus: Designing for Care" builds on this foundation to explore the role of architecture in culturally foregrounding and valuing care work. Authored by Jahn and Rafi Segal, this essay marshals artistic spatial practices, architecture, and urbanism in a discussion of their joint project called Carehaus, the United States' first intergenerational care-based cohousing project. Together with their third partner, developer Ernst Valery, Jahn and Segal organized codesign sessions with caregivers, care receivers, physicians, and nurses to create a new architecture of equity and solidarity among care providers and care receivers.

The essay "Architecture for New Collectives" authored by Segal, further exemplifies architecture's role in promoting and shaping solidarity. Drawing on his experience in designing spaces for kibbutz communities in Israel, cohousing typologies, and collective neighborhoods in rural Rwanda, Segal describes how the process of creating organizational structures and protocols to manage mutualized resources can produce new collective identities and spaces. This process can be initiated through bottom-up self-organized groups, top-down government or public-sector institutions, or some combination thereof.

Rwanda, one of Africa's smallest yet most densely populated and progressive countries, has a topography dominated by hills and mountains. The population, currently predominantly young and rural, has long developed communities along slopes vulnerable to landslides. To address the country's need for better-built low-cost housing for families displaced by natural disasters, a team of MIT students led by Segal collaborated with the Rwanda Housing Authority, the University of Rwanda, and local brick manufacturers. The collaboration also centrally involved local residents who were trained in bricklaying and then afterward paid to help build homes for future neighbors. Through its structural system and embedded gradient brick patterns, the house they designed offers natural ventilation, greater control over privacy, flexibility in interior partitioning, variable covered indoor and outdoor spaces, and a front porch that serves as a space for family-scale commerce. These factors were determined through discussions and design mock-ups of various brick patterns forming the house walls. In essence, the design of the prototype house and *how* participants engaged in its construction proved equally critical to fostering solidarity: new alliances between previously unconnected regional and international institutions fostered back-and-forth learning and welcomed future inhabitants into the community.

When mutual aid flourishes to overcome an infrastructural collapse or neglect, participants who share and build new resources retain these ways of working together. Drawing

A new affordable housing model for rural land, Mageragere, Rwanda, 2018. An MIT design workshop led by Rafi Segal worked with masons, local brick manufacturers, villagers, and students from MIT and Rwanda University to design-build a low-cost prototype house. Photo by Rafi Segal.

Students from MIT and the University
of Rwanda lay bricks together with
villagers in the construction of a new
affordable village house for Rwanda's
rural land, Mageragere, outskirts of
Kigali, Rwanda, 2018. Photo by
Ben Segal.

on human connections and learned skills, participants bolster their resilience to forestall or weather future crises. In this way, giving structure to these networks and pathways is an act of design.

In 2008, a dozen preteens and adults from a low-income community in rural Honduras reached out to Jahn to collaborate on creative approaches to literacy, which was, in their words, the number one way to "lift them out of their poverty cycle."[5] To instill a culture of storytelling as solidarity, Jahn and the community invented the idea of a bandit who *eats* stories and pesters little kids. To appease Bibliobandido's insatiable appetite and thus avert general calamity, youth would nourish him with stories they'd written.

Captivated, youth equipped with the power of imagination began enacting the legend of Bibliobandido (Story Eater) on a monthly basis with nineteen surrounding communities. Ritualizing their triumph over their beloved story-hungry villain over the next decade, and still on-going today, participants young and old have woven an elaborate, fantastical cosmology whose allure rivals Santa Claus. Designing a project so that youth saw themselves as co-creators and as legend-bearers entailed a number of intentional aesthetic considerations informing the creation of costumes, artifacts, and how we engage others.[6]

In the example of Bibliobandido, the solidarity formed through shared world-building contributed to what Sarah Szanton, dean of Johns Hopkins School of Nursing, might refer to as structural resilience, or the "resilience and reserve developed in communities and neighborhoods . . . [such as] religious communities, mutual aid societies, greenspace, family tradition, and Historically Black College/University attendance."[7] Underscoring the importance of mutualism in social movements, authors Sara Horowitz, Nathan Schneider, Dean Spade, among others suggest that social movements grow as participants forge intersectional alliances, advocate

Bibliobandido (Story Eater), the story-eating bandit created by Marisa Morán Jahn and the community of El Pital, Honduras. Photo by Marisa Morán Jahn, featuring Koqui Alvarez.

Youth in rural Honduras who have carried on the living legend of Bibliobandido, the story-eating villain, since 2010. Photo by Marisa Morán Jahn.

for systemic change, and gain awareness of the history of structural inequality perpetuating injustices.

Adding to this discourse, the Bibliobandido literacy movement points to the power of shared *imagination* in animating forms of structural resilience: Here, design enables the shaping of a collective narrative that strengthens community. As Silvia Federici reminds us, "Reproduction does not only concern our material needs—such as housing, food preparation, the organization of space, childrearing, sex, and procreation. An important aspect of it is the reproduction of our collective memory and the cultural symbols that give meaning to our life and nourish our struggles."[8] Consider *Arabian Nights*, a "reproduction" written by many individuals over many continents and millennia: while each adaptation of the frame tale bears the marks of its political and cultural inflections, key figures incarnate the durability of a vivid shared cultural imaginary. A. S. Byatt fittingly uses the figure of the genie to allegorize the story's appeal and transmutation across ages: "Genies are immortal beings, who can break the ineluctable rules of time and space in which humans are trapped. . . . Genes, like genies, are potentially immortal, and carry language and the imagination from generation to generation, like the infinitely renewed, metamorphosing life of [Arabian] Nights."[9] In other words, the act of creation—storytelling, in this case—activates values and ignites the imagination to transcend the present. By corollary, to withstand those forces seeking its destruction, mutualism therefore needs creativity.

Toward Pluri-economies

In the United States, mutualism has surged in the past decade in reaction to sharpening economic precarity brought on by the neoliberal privatization of essential life resources as well as by a growing mistrust of government and public institutions.

Because they provide a necessary mode of economic and social resilience, mutual aid groups historically surge during times of crises.[10] As we've seen during the Covid pandemic, it's precisely these moments of larger government- or market-based failure that make visible the vast array of interdependent, mutualistic practices cohering our everyday lives.

To name a few examples, informal networks and platform cooperatives enable us to share rides, vehicles, beds, and skills. Time banks, care banks, and seed banks enable us to "bank" labor or resources for future generations or for times when we need them. Gift economies and favors allow us to share abundances. Formal and informal commoning—sometimes referred to as common pool resources and common pool regimes (CPRs)—enables individuals to share resources (produce, eggs, easements, waterways, land) and access (hunting, fishing, swimming, harvesting). A variety of financial institutions (credit unions, informal lending circles) provide low- or no-interest ways to bank. Early settlers in the United States built barns by pooling labor. Around the world, historical equivalents to barn-raising include *bayanihan* in the Philippines and *dugnat* in Finland—that enable labor-intensive architectural practices to be shared.[11]

At this point, skeptics could respond by comparing these examples of mutualism to "*the* capitalist (commodity) market." This maneuver solipsistically adheres to the capitalist playbook by reinforcing a monoversal understanding of the world, blindly ignoring that capitalist commodity exchange is but *one* form of economization. Relatedly, we therefore avoid using the phrase *alternative economies* which centers capitalism and marginalizes everything else. Another common knee-jerk reaction outlined in the capitalist playbook is to assume that the only other way to challenge the capitalocentric world is by a revolution. This drastically simplified binary ignores the many changes that can already be made in the present tense and the complexity of today's economies.

In this book, we and others point out that mutualist practices work in manifold ways—with and against capitalism's very existence. For example, co-ops—which have long proliferated around the world—are formally defined as business entities whose fiscal structures prioritizes the needs of their workers and their communities over individual profit. Jessica Gordon Nembhard notes that co-ops in the United States employ 2.1 million people and contribute an estimated $154 billion to the country's total income. The jobs created by co-ops provide higher wages than those in investor-oriented firms, and the revenue earned by cooperatives is more likely to stay in the communities where they originate.[12] Additionally, co-ops dedicate more resources toward training, skill sharing, and building diverse pipelines for marginalized individuals who then apply these skills in other domains. As several conversations in this book discuss, co-ops provide a stabilizing force and proliferate during periods of volatility, as seen in the recent Covid pandemic.

Given their importance to society as a whole, why, then, are co-ops marginalized within contemporary discourse and the public imaginary? Schneider points out that after World War II, a reactionary fear of communism led most larger co-ops in the United States (e.g., Best Western motels, Land O'Lakes dairy, Dairy Queen, Associated Press, and Visa) to blend into the corporate order. "Vulnerable as they were to Red-baiting, democratic [cooperative] businesses cast themselves as good-ole American capitalism."[13] It's helpful to historicize the reasons why co-ops unfortunately but perhaps necessarily adjusted their public image in the mid-twentieth century; doing so helps us to fully recognize a shift in values today, when 80 percent of Americans have said they would choose a cooperative over an investor-owned corporate brand.[14] Here, design can play a key role in updating our spatial environment and cultural imaginary to reflect today's valorization of what economic geographers J. K. Gibson-Graham refer to as community-centered economies.[15]

Besides co-ops, many other mutualist, informal, and nonmonetized economies directly contribute to and enable capitalist economies. Our collaborator Ai-jen Poo, former executive director and now board president of NDWA, has helped build a movement to strengthen the socioeconomic justice of nannies, housekeepers, and caregivers while expanding options for all those who need care. As Poo discusses with us in this book, care is a form of labor that makes all other work possible: to go to work and participate in the workforce, wage-earning adults rely on a patchwork of paid care workers and unpaid family caregivers to look after their loved ones, young and old. In monetary terms, the United States' forty million largely *unpaid* family caregivers provide upward of $470 billion worth of unpaid services to family members.[16] Yet, as physician Dhruv Khullar points out, family caregivers who leave the workforce lose hundreds of thousands of dollars in wages and benefits over their lifetime and experience disproportionate challenges to their own physical and mental health.[17] In other words, on a global scale, caregivers—a workforce comprised largely of women of color—absorb both the body burdens[18] and the willful financial negligence of advanced capitalism.

After working for years in the Philippines' Department of Agrarian Reform and later in tourism, Erlinda Alvarez immigrated to Chicago to work as a caregiver for older adults. "In the Philippines, we take pride in how well we care for our old people. I think that's why we come to places like America: to get paid for our care while helping to improve poverty back home."[19] Erlinda, known for being joyous, immediately brightens when asked if she can share her superpowers as a caregiver. "My special talent is my voice. I like to sing to the people I care for because it brings people together. Singing to those

Created by Marisa Morán Jahn with the National Domestic Workers Alliance and Caring Across Generations, *CareForce* (2010–) is a public art project amplifying the voices of the fastest-growing workforce in the United States—caregivers. A mobile studio designed by Jahn, the *CareForce One*, convenes caregivers and care-receivers to share resources and stories. Shown here, the CareForce One helped to animate public space and increase the visibility of a rally for economic justice on the steps of Los Angeles City Hall led by local domestic worker groups. Photo by Marc Shavitz.

Carehaus, the United States' first intergenerational care-based co-housing project whose first prototype is built in Baltimore, Maryland. Designed by Rafi Segal in collaboration with Marisa Morán Jahn.

who have lost their memory opens a new door; they are surprised—and comforted—to be able to access their previous life." She sings a few songs but then suddenly breaks down in tears, recalling the many humiliations she endured on the job. "If I had known how shameful this work would be I would not have come to the U.S.—but now I'm stuck here and my family back home relies on my wages." Nearing what in the United States would be considered retirement age, Erlinda is not much younger than those for whom she cares. "I worry what will happen to me when I get older," she says. "Some of us even die while caring for others. It costs thousands and thousands of dollars to ship the body back home by plane to the Philippines so that it can be buried according to our culture's customs. Can you imagine having to struggle in life *and* in death?"[20]

Erlinda's story exposes how capitalism's indices fail to capture the care economies it relies upon and in doing so, furthers the global feminization and racialization of poverty. For example, while the GDP measures the monetary or market value of all the finished goods and services of a given country, a more apt financial instrument might capture the *interdependence* of capitalist and care economies. In other words, Erlinda's story captures the stark structural asymmetries of this global "curo-sphere"—the labor, the push-pull dynamics of immigration, and the statecraft involved in managing and financing care.[21] Through this example, we see how a capitalocentric mindset has predominated in shaping not only our urban spaces, policies, and cultural imaginaries as well as their inability to fully capture the totality of our economic reality.

Theorists such as J. K. Gibson-Graham exhort the need for a new *language* that "expands our economic *vocabulary*, widening the identity of the economy to include all of those practices excluded or marginalized by a strong theory of capitalism" (italics added).[22] This logocentric bias suffuses Gibson-Graham's emphasis that change occurs within *discursive* shifts: "Diverse *languages* of economy already exist but are rendered ineffectual by the hegemony of capitalocentrism. They have . . . [subsisted] in the shadows of mainstream economic thinking. To produce a potential dislocation of the hegemony of capitalocentric *discourse*, we need to identify and begin to liberate these alternative languages from their *discursive* subordination" (italics added).[23]

As an artist and an architect, we demand more than simply *language* to reimagine solidarity. Building on Gibson-Graham's seminal notion of diverse economies and utilizing Arturo Escobar's concept of the "pluriverse"—"a world where many worlds fit"—we refer to a totality of community-centered economies *alongside* capitalist practices as "pluri-economies." By surfacing the pluri-economies that aptly describe our everyday life, we can begin to properly design for them. Further, the notion of pluri-economies operates as an essential framework to anchor design for mutualistic values in society. The concept of pluri-economies thus enables us to center solidarity as a concrete design opportunity informing our current socio-economic-political reality.

In our era when the lines between private and public sectors blur, many current mutual aid initiatives become problematic when they absolve the government of its shortcomings: In other words, why are private citizens doing the government's job, and why should the state be let off the hook as a result? *The notion of pluri-economies, however, recognizes that the government's roles and responsibilities need to be redefined to enable mutualism to flourish.* Key questions arise that we must address: Should the government regulate the gig economy and ensure a transparent and equitable digital marketplace for gig workers? As an essential utility, should digital broadband be government-regulated like water? How do these policies and others empower communities? And what are other ways in which government can support mutualism?

Design as Dialogue

As discussed in the preceding sections, our imperative to design *for*, *with*, and *through* solidarity resituates with whom we work, how we work, and how we can design beyond capitalocentric conventions. When designers recognize their axiological (moral) agency, traditional client-designer or commissioner-artist relationships shift: designers expand their role beyond servicing the demands of a private client or institution, identifying new kinds of user-participants and processes. This re-constellation of power can be described as a more horizontal formation of equal parties based on partner relationships and respect for the individual skills, talents, diversity, and lived experiences we each bring. In no way does this reduce the scope and involvement of the designer; on the contrary, it allows the designer to fully engage and contribute their skill set.

The notion of design solidarity also asks us to recognize that involving design only in the *execution* of solutions is simply not enough: stopping there would deny the grace, poiesis, and imaginative force that creativity confers. To this we add that designing solidarity necessarily takes place as a dialogue between form and (collective) self-trans*form*ation.

With this ethos in mind, this book emerged as a series of dialogues—conversations with cross-sector practitioners with whom we engage in mutual learning around the relationship between design and solidarity.

Duke University professor and political philosopher Michael Hardt understands the commons as a third space existing between the private and public and shaped by a multitude. The making of the commons has become all the more urgent in counteracting vagaries of the gig economy and pandemic-induced economic precarity.

An activist-researcher from Cali, Colombia, working on territorial struggles, Arturo Escobar introduces the concept of *redes* (in English, *nets*), a dynamic self-organized network of support and solidarity that holds a community together. Designing for the pluriverse, he suggests, requires recognizing and designing for epistemic differences. Further, designing for the future involves crafting alternatives in the present.

The cooperative movement has been critiqued for its focus on white, liberal, and upper-middle-class values that fail to capture the solidarity economy already thriving among immigrant and BIPOC communities and across the Global South. In her groundbreaking work, economist and Africana scholar Jessica Gordon Nembhard unearths an important yet largely hidden precedent for today's solidarity economy— the Underground Railroad. By pooling economic resources, knowledge, and assets, antebellum Black mutual networks enabled enslaved people to escape and seek freedom in the North. Nembhard urges us to seize the power of collectivizing and humbly recognize the rich resources we each can offer.

Seeking solutions to address the inequalities pronounced by a profit-driven gig economy, scholar-activist Trebor Scholz, founding director of the Institute for the Cooperative Digital Economy at The New School, argues for the importance of platform cooperatives. Cooperatives, he suggests, do not replace capitalist enterprises but instead function as critical supplements that effectively withstand economic crises, organize geographically dispersed freelancers, and strengthen workers' rights.

Journalist and futurist Greg Lindsay outlines how the Covid pandemic has led to an explosion of mutual aid groups that differ from their predecessors in two important ways. First, the virus's global scale resulted in the simultaneous appearance of hundreds of different local groups, each with their own aims and constituencies. Second, the nature of the virus, coupled with quarantines and lockdowns, means that for communities with broadband access, these networks often appropriate online productivity tools as a first step toward organizing. Through conversations with technologists, practitioners, and citizen-activists, Lindsay asks how these mutual aid networks and collectives can evolve to harness the physical and the digital, what we can we learn from their digital-first strategies, and what cannot be replicated digitally.

Social entrepreneur Mercedes Bidart unpacks the genesis and implications of Quipu, the digital marketplace she codesigned with residents of Barranquilla, Colombia, a region where 70 percent of the inhabitants are resettled survivors of armed conflict. Using a digital platform that enables community members to barter and build creditworthiness, Quipu demonstrates the power of the solidarity economy to combat cash shortfalls and liquidity crises. Bidart also discusses the role that architectural and urban-scale design can play in strengthening digital platforms today.

Ai-jen Poo discusses the United States' care crisis and the urgent need to mutualize care. The pandemic has brought awareness of care as a form of commons benefiting a population majority that relies on domestic labor. Art, architecture, and stories help galvanize both the movement for domestic workers' rights and society's need for consistent, quality care.

The conversations and essays within this book exemplify the dialogical nature of design solidarity in practice.

Notes

1. Dolores Hayden, *The Grand Domestic Revolution: A History of Feminist Designs for American Homes, Neighborhoods, and Cities* (Cambridge, MA: MIT Press, 1982).
2. "Our Story," Movers and Shakers, accessed December 22, 2021, https://www.moversandshakersnyc.com/our-story.
3. Led by Marisa Morán Jahn, Team NannyVan most often included Anjum Asharia, Marc Shavitz, and Anya Krawcheck. Other frequent NannyVan allies included Guillermina Castellanos, Narbada Chhetri, Christine Lewis, Namrata Pradhan, Meches Rosales, Jules Rochielle Sievert, Natalicia Tracy, Barbara Young, and members of the National Domestic Workers Alliance, including its executive director, Ai-jen Poo. Steve Shada is the brilliant mind who "MacGyvered" the NannyVan from seven junkyards.
4. Paraphasing the Anti-Defamation League, in the last few years, the term "DREAMer" has been used to describe young undocumented immigrants who were brought to the United States as children where they have lived, attended school, and in many cases, identify as American. The term DREAMer originally took its name from the bill in Congress, but it has a double meaning suggestive of the aspirations of undocumented youth for a better future. "What Is the Dream Act and Who Are the Dreamers?," Anti-Defamation League, accessed December 23, 2021, https://www.adl.org/education/educator-resources/lesson-plans/what-is-the-dream-act-and-who-are-the-dreamers.

5. Daniel Rodriguez, interview by Marisa Morán Jahn, Arizona State University, Phoenix, 2014.

6. Equal parts wonder and civic empowerment, the Bibliobandido public art and literacy movement has since reached over twenty thousand individuals across Central and North America, including, as of 2022, New York's Brooklyn Public Library system and its sixty-four branches. As a whole, the project broadens what art can be and do.

7. Elly Goetz, interview by Marisa Morán Jahn, El Pital, El Pital, Honduras, March 16, 2008.

8. LaFave, S. E., Bandeen-Roche, K., Gee, G., Thorpe, R. J., Li, Q., Crews, D., Samuel, L., Cooke, A., Hladek, M., and Szanton, S. L. "Quantifying Older Black Americans' Exposure to Structural Racial Discrimination: How Can We Measure the Water in Which We Swim?" In press, *Journal of Urban Health* (2022).

9. Silvia Federici, *Re-enchanting the World: Feminism and the Politics of the Commons* (Oakland, CA: PM Press, 2019), 5.

10. A. S. Byatt, introduction to *The Arabian Nights: Tales from a Thousand and One Nights*, trans. Richard Francis Burton (New York: Modern Library, 2001), xiv.

11. In "Eight Facts About Cooperative Enterprise," Jessica Gordon Nembhard points out that "cooperative businesses have lower failure rates than other businesses, both after the first year (10 percent failure versus 60–80 percent) and after five years (90 percent still operating versus 3–5 percent). Evidence also shows that cooperatives successfully address the effects of economic crisis and survive crisis better." In Trebor Scholz and Nathan Schneider, eds., *Ours to Hack and to Own: The Rise of Platform Cooperativism, a New Vision for the Future of Work and a Fairer Internet* (New York: O/R Books, 2017), 29.

12. Nathan Schneider, *Everything for Everyone: The Radical Tradition That Is Shaping the Next Economy* (New York: Nation Books, 2018), 8–9.

13. In "Eight Facts About Cooperative Enterprise," Nembhard notes that for every $1,000 spent at a food co-op, $1,606 goes to the local economy; for every $1 million in sales, 9.3 jobs are created. In Scholz and Schneider, *Ours to Hack*, 30.

14. Schneider, *Everything for Everyone*, 6.

15. Schneider, *Everything for Everyone*, 8–9.

16. See J. K. Gibson-Graham, *A Postcapitalist Politics* (Minneapolis: University of Minnesota Press, 2006) and *End of Capitalism (As We Knew It): A Feminist Critique of Political Economy* (Minneapolis: University of Minnesota Press, 2006).

17. Susan C. Reinhard, Lynn Friss Feinberg, Ari Houser, Rita Choula, and Molly Evans, *Valuing the Invaluable: 2019 Update Charting a Path Forward* (Washington, DC: AARP Public Policy Institute, 2019), https://www.aarp.org/content/dam/aarp/ppi/2019/11/valuing-the -invaluable-2019-update-charting-a-path-forward.doi.10.26419 -2Fppi.00082.001.pdf.
18. Dhruv Khullar, "Who Will Care for the Caregivers," *New York Times*, January 19, 2017, https://www.nytimes.com/2017/01/19/upshot/who -will-care-for-the-caregivers.html.
19. In *A Billion Black Anthropocenes or None* (Minneapolis: University of Minnesota Press, 2019), Kathryn Yusoff discusses the biopolitical dimensions of global resource extraction. Here, we borrow Yusoff's translation of these geopolitical tensions into embodiment to discuss the ways that women of color working as caregivers disproportion- ately "absorb" the externalities of late capitalism.
20. Erlinda Alvarez, interview by Marisa Morán Jahn, North Chicago, Illinois, February 16, 2015.
21. Marisa Morán Jahn and Rafi Segal, "Towards an Architecture of Care," in "Structures of Mutual Support: Beyond," catalogue for the Philip- pines Pavilion at the 17th Biennale di Architettura, ed. Kahdka and Furunes, *2021*.
22. Hironori Onuki, "Care, Social (Re)production and Global Labour Migration: Japan's 'Special Gift' Toward 'Innately Gifted' Filipino Workers," *New Political Economy* 14, no. 4 (2009): 489–516, https:// doi.org/10.1080/13563460903287306.
23. Gibson-Graham, *A Postcapitalist Politics*, 57.
24. Gibson-Graham, *A Postcapitalist Politics*, 60.

Conversations

On the Common

Michael Hardt

Editorial note: Many contributors to this book—including ourselves—refer to shared assets and resources as "the commons." However, in our conversation with Michael Hardt and in his scholarship, he uses this phrase in the singular ("the common"). As Hardt previously wrote in *Multitude: War and Democracy in the Age of Empire*, a book coauthored with Antonio Negri, "[We are reluctant to use the phrase] 'the commons' because that term refers to pre-capitalist-shared spaces that were destroyed by the advent of private property. Although more awkward, "the common" highlights the philosophical content of the term and emphasizes that this is not a return to the past but a new development."[1] Therefore, in keeping with Hardt and Negri's intentional use of the phrase, and to avoid switching between the plural and singular of the word, we've used the phrase "the common" in the singular.

Designing the Common

Rafi: To start the conversation, can you give us a brief definition of "the common" or perhaps a way to visualize where or how the common exists?

> **Michael:** When I think about the common, I divide it into two categories as a starting point. I think of the common first as the earth and its ecosystems: all the

things that we share and that we are forced to share. What falls into this category? The earth itself, the atmosphere, the water, the land, etc. This first notion of the common is the one that has been the source of so many problems derived from its partitioning through property and through state control.

The second notion of the common is the commonwealth that we produce through our own creativity. Think of intellectual production—the production of images, of code, of scientific knowledge, and of music. These are all things that ought to be common. In fact, they are things that are *more productive* as common. We get more out of them this way. When they are made private or controlled by the state, we run into restrictions, obstacles, and blockages.

So this is perhaps a cursory way to begin thinking about things: the common that we discover and the common we create. It's a false distinction, which quickly breaks down, and the two are always mixed, but it can be a helpful initial distinction.

Marisa: In *Multitude*, you write, "The common we share, in fact, is not so much discovered, as it is produced." What role does design play in the effective management of shared resources? And how can design help reinforce ideas about the common?

Michael: All practices of self-governance require a designed structure. So I think that even to agree upon any shared understanding of the common we need a designed structure for deliberation in order to define these terms. The structures by which we communicate with each other are foundational for the democratic management of the common. In other words, design and architecture, considered in a very broad sense, are essential processes to the sustainability of the common.

Rafi: Can you say more about the role of design as a form of maintaining and sustaining the common?

Michael: Design comes into play in this process of democratic decision-making and democracy at large. In the grand scheme, we need to position democratic decision-making as an activity that happens from the smallest scale—such as the neighborhood and single dwelling—to the largest scale—like the metropolis or the nation.

Scale and Solidarity

Rafi: I'd like to ask you about what you mean by *scale*— from the household to the metropolis, as you say. Can you talk about the relationship between scale and your concept of the multitude?

Michael: For the last decades, the question of scale has been a major question for social movements. This is largely because movements themselves have been, especially since 2011, focused on very specific and local questions. Think about the *Indignados* anti-austerity protests in Spain that started in May of 2011. Protesters had neighborhood-based *comisiones* (working groups) about sexual violence, gentrification, and so forth. They were superrooted in the local. And yet, when one recognizes the extension of a cycle of struggles, one can recognize how these same movements scale up. At the very least, we recognize their extensive international, if not global, effects.

On the Common

For instance, when I think of the contagion, inspiration, or spread of movements, I trace contagious lineages: in 2011, social upheaval in Tunisia and Egypt, to Spain and Greece, to Occupy Wall Street, to various other Occupy movements; then in 2013, Turkey and Brazil and Hong Kong. This is a kind of extension at a global or international scale of something that's intensely rooted in the local.

My first approach to this notion of scaling up, then, is through the international cycle of struggles. You could also think of this concept in viral terms as a kind of contagion mechanism, where movements that have very specific and local conditions are nonetheless able to communicate beyond them. And in doing so, they communicate a repertoire of practices, like encampment or general assembly. They could even communicate a set of aspirations.

Marisa: While this "repertoire of practices" enables a scaling up, might they also strengthen solidarity within the collective?

Michael: Well, within the collectives, one of the most important mandates, it seems to me, is about multiplicity. The most powerful social movements of the last two decades—for example, Occupy Wall Street or the Gilets Jaunes—maintain a constant internal critique that insists on multiplicity and demands equality in terms of race, gender, sexuality, class, ability, and more. That is not to say that these movements have successfully established intersectional practices. Certainly not! But they have constantly criticized themselves for these shortcomings. And those internal critiques are a symptom of an as yet unrealized political desire. The political must be thought of in terms of multiplicity.

Conversations

Conversations

Social movements must recognize multiple axes of domination and operate on various fronts of struggle simultaneously.

Marisa: Can you say more about the intersectional challenge of multiplicity as solidarity formation?

Michael: Solidarity, even international solidarity, has traditionally been a concept by which one recognizes the flexibility, extensions, and limits of a common struggle. Lately, I've been interested in internal critiques of solidarity, both international and grassroots. I'm thinking particularly of Rosa Luxemburg who, in 1905, after the rebellion and insurrection in Russia poignantly critiqued her German comrades as they expressed solidarity for the poor, suffering Russians as if they were in a completely different world. She pointed out that her German comrades had failed to recognize that the struggle of the Russians was an intimate chapter of their own political history. It's not that she is somehow against international solidarity. On the contrary! What Rosa Luxemburg was emphasizing was that pious or partial solidarity for other people's struggles is insufficient. For Luxemburg, solidarity is not empathy for others but rather the recognition that other people's struggles are part of your own struggle.

Here is another historical example. In the 1970s, there were numerous examples across Europe and the United States of feminists who were criticizing socialist comrades. They were criticizing male socialists—and not just the misogynist ones (of which there are plenty) but the ones who expressed their solidarity for the feminist movement. These women said, "What you don't recognize is that our struggle against patriarchy is really internal to *your* struggle against capital. It's not like you should think of it as some separate thing that you have sympathy for. It's really part of what you're doing. It *has* to be part of what you're doing."

I think that's the way of understanding today's political struggles founded on multiplicity. It's not like I can be involved in struggles about gender equality and ignore those who are in an antiracist struggle. You have to recognize instead that antiracist struggles are internal to your own struggle to recognize how the structures of domination of white supremacy, patriarchy, and capital are intimate and co-constitutive. Our struggles have to recognize their own internal connections. I think this is a tall order, but it's what's involved in scaling up or, better yet, scaling out into different terrains of struggle. We have to recognize their intimate and internal connections.

Rafi: Connecting this now to design, a lot of struggles today are formed or cast in terms of protest—which is necessary and right. At the same time, every struggle also has to create a solid social alternative. Actually, struggles need to create the *imagination* of a social alternative to spark ideas about *real* structures. What challenges does the multitude encounter in building these imaginaries?

Michael: Once one recognizes the function of multiplicity in revolt, one has to then ask the question of whether or not a multiplicity can actually act politically. Traditional notions of political action have always involved a centralized intelligence, whether it be the party, the vanguard, or the class.

We are challenged when we are required to confront and recognize the coherent and lasting forms of political action of a multitude. So far I've expressed this idea with regard to contemporary social movements. However, we might also need to broadly recognize the coherence of *common action* within a multiplicity.

I pose this in more philosophical terms because, in some way, this is about recognizing the nature or organization of the common in general. How can we have a multiplicity of subjectivities that are able to use and make decisions about the social wealth that we share? The political problem is similar here.

Marisa: Perhaps the answer is what we touched upon earlier: democracy as a process of design. But we might add a proviso to emphasize its evolving role: "Democracy necessarily involves a process of *iterative* design." As the shifting needs of a multitude change and as the common itself changes, so too, design must necessarily change.

The Sharing Economy

Rafi: How do these notions of the common relate to the distinctions between the public versus the private? For example, you make the helpful suggestion that the common is a space between these two. Why do you see this third space as the most urgent one to tend to?

Michael: Property is becoming increasingly problematic today—both private and public property. And I see two main things that both private and public property share: first, an exclusive usage and, second, a monopoly of decision-making. It often seems as though we have no alternative between those two— as if there can be only private property or alternately public property controlled by the state or some governmental body. But in reality, there are many aspects of our lives that are neither public nor private. This is where we find the common. It's the opposite of property—private property and public property—in those two senses. On the one hand, it involves open access rather than exclusive access. And on the other hand, rather than a monopoly of decision-making, managing the common involves a democratic scheme of decision-making.

This last idea seems to me the crucial part that is often missing in discussions—or even in imaginations—of making things common. We need to think more about the things we *could* share and *how* we could share them. For many people, there's a belief that after one single disagreement, any system for sharing could spontaneously falter. In the long run, both sharing and creating democratic management are hugely challenging endeavors—but ones that we have to face today.

Marisa: Today we are seeing examples of top-down "sharing" that neither require nor in fact obviate an internal connection, shared struggle, and solidarity. Those aspects of the sharing economy connote a corporate, profit-driven structure that ignores the principles of self-determination and autonomy. We have hope that mutualistic societies that arose around the Covid pandemic might broaden or introduce new ways of sharing. Is it naïve or polyannaish to advocate for more basic forms of sharing?

Michael: It's incredible how the central terms of our political vocabulary have all become corrupted. Terms like *democracy* and *freedom*, which used to be at the center of liberation projects, have been so corrupted that they almost seem unusable. It is an important task of political theory, I think, to give these terms new meanings. Perhaps the same is true of *sharing*. Sharing now means "I will capitalize on the extra bedroom in my house" or "I'll capitalize on the use of my car." I think it would be an excellent project to recuperate what sharing *could* mean. A little bit of my indignation is that this degraded notion of sharing rubs against what I had previously understood sharing to mean, so part of me wonders if we first have to recuperate what sharing meant *before*.

That said, maybe the solution is to invent something that stands apart so that we could use the sharing economy in its various forms as a counterpoint. We could recognize the injustices and exploitations involved in "sharing" and use this knowledge as a kind of launchpad for reimagining what a real sharing economy could be—an economy that doesn't involve exploiting each other in the most minute forms of our daily life. Instead, it could actually allow for sharing as an act of open cooperation and collaboration with others. Sharing could help create and sustain relationships based on equality and freedom. That is what we ought to aim for. If it were based on these values, I would love for a sharing economy to be in place. And that in itself—this notion of a *real* sharing economy—could be the foundation for thinking of collective economic autonomy and self-governance as well as the other ways we could organize our collective lives.

Note

1. Michael Hardt and Antonio Negri, *Multitude: War and Democracy in the Age of Empire* (New York: Penguin, 2004), xv.

On the Common

On Self-Determination in a World Where Many Worlds Fit

Arturo Escobar

Marisa: To start off the conversation, could you tell us about your concept of *redes* and the fieldwork and ideas that led you to it?

> **Arturo:** I first started thinking about this question of *redes* in the 1990s when I was working on *Territories of Difference*, a book about how people struggle to defend their territory on the Pacific coast of Colombia. I was spending time with Black activists who were part of Proceso de Comunidades Negras (Black Communities' Process), otherwise known as PCN. I was documenting and thinking about the ways in which people struggle to defend their territories and ways of life. This rain-forest region of Colombia is an incredibly biodiverse aquatic space, shaped by streams, rivers, the sea, humidity, rain, and mangroves alike. Everywhere you go you inevitably run into *redes*, which literally translates to "nets used for fishing." You see them all around you: laying on the shore, perhaps abandoned because they have become damaged; in the hands of someone who is repairing them; or in the hands of someone who is building a *red* from the start.
>
> In my contact with PCN, I found that this term *redes* was also ubiquitous in political discourse to describe what Anglo-American academics call networks. There was a period of organizing in the 1990s in the Colombia's Pacific coast region when black

communities, peasant organizations, women's groups, indigenous organizations, and other groups started to use the term *redes* to describe the self-organized mesh-like relations that emerged as their local and regional organizing became interlinked with national and transnational struggles. This led me to research the network theories that had been emerging in the 1990s in Anglo-American academia and to start questioning how the *redes* I was seeing actually interacted with network theory. My suspicion was that there was something far more subtle, nuanced, and richer that was happening when referring to *redes* and its association with meshes.

Rafi: In what way does redes stand out, and what theories did you compare it to?

Arturo: At the time, *redes* was a counterpoint to the emerging network theories and to the actor-network approach as understood by Bruno Latour. For Latour, the real is the result of networks of multiple actors and actants that come together to generate a somewhat identifiable and singular world. In *redes*, I saw something that was more chaotic, mysterious, and expansive than the anthropocentric, "practical" theories being discussed. As an anthropologist, I examined ethnographic approaches to networks that see them as the products of movements/phenomena—in particular, social phenomena where people come together to promote causes, advocate change, and restructure power. Most network theories and theories of assemblages, as well as traditional anthropological readings of them, still operated through a Euclidean geometry: networks composed of fixed points and/or nodes that are connected by lines of relations. I felt this conventional geometry was far too rigid.

Gilles Deleuze and Félix Guattari's notion of the rhizomatic was definitely an influence on me.[1] Here, there was a more heterogeneous approach where rhizomes grow in "unplanned" directions depending on the concrete, political, physical, and affective circumstances encountered. It's a far more sensitive and ecological approach and definitely less Euclidean—as they say, rhizomes are more like a patchwork of juxtaposed pieces that can be joined together in manifold ways, a sort of Riemannian geometry. This metaphor was also a precursor to a biological turn in network theory, originating in theories of emergence and self-organization, that made more room for disorderly or at least semiorderly behaviors. *Redes* was my attempt to be less prescriptive. I tried instead to attend to a nascent, "living-breathing" sense of enmeshment whose mutability could have daily retransfigurations. I wanted to prioritize surprise and haphazard forms of intelligences—the interventions of life itself.

Marisa: How do you see this approach to *redes* as part of your idea of future and/or reality producing?

Arturo: I think critical social theory has been doing damage control on the very narrow descriptions of reality that we've inherited from traditional philosophy. There's the modern view that things exist in and of themselves. Through this lens, everything functions as an individual or intrinsically existing entity in a universe that is filled with similar entities and that operates as a neutral container. But this is a huge distortion—things are far more interconnected and interdependent. This is continually proven by physics and ecology and has been the indigenous cosmological vision of the world for far longer. It's a more radical view—one that sees the continuity and interdependence of all things. The southern African concept of *ubuntu* beautifully describes the idea of interconnection in a very intimate way. To put it simply, *ubuntu* suggests that because I exist, you exist, and that because everything exists, I exist. This "everything" includes humans and nonhumans alike.

Rafi: How is the concept of *redes* important in making change today? How can it transform our perspective of the world?

Arturo: More and more people are coming together to suggest that the contemporary ecological crisis today is in fact also a crisis in our way or model of thinking. Like I said, we are in a stage of repairing the insidious violences and damages of dualist thought. Today, what we optimistically call postdualist social theory disempowers these modes of thought that have led to alienation and isolation. We are trying to reconnect, but we know it's not a matter of drawing lines. That's why I find *redes* to be such a fantastic concept: *redes* require interlacing, weaving, and restructuring.

In Spanish, the word for weaving is *tejer*, and something that has been woven is a *tejido*, which is the same word used to describe the tissues of the body. Our bodies are woven together. When our wounds heal, it is because our *tejidos* are healing. When I think of the repair/healing work that has to be done to rectify the ontological, political, and environmental damage of dualism, I often use the phrase "healers of the web of life." We need to heal and reweave the web of life so that life can continue to flow. From a "pluriversal" perspective, life is in ceaseless transformation—always open and always flowing. It is a flow of shapes, forms, relations, intensities, and futures. The *tejidos* and *redes* built by many groups of people today struggling against objectifying and "monoversal" modes of existence are conducive to life. What makes me hopeful is that *redes* are continually being remade and repaired by multiple others in variegated, localized ways.

Marisa: This seems like a vision of the world and life where care is central. In some way, care is what maintains the flow that you're describing through the maintenance of *redes*.

Arturo: Yes, caretaking, restoring, refashioning, reusing, remaking, regenerating, resurgence. The weavers of life don't just preserve life as it is. They channel it onward. It's an ethics that requires new or, rather, renewed practices/politics.

Transition Design

Rafi: With this in mind, could we talk a bit about your use of the concept *transition design*? So far we have a sense of the things that you are working *against* when it comes to dualism and breakage. I'd love to hear you speak about the things you view as essential for us to move toward—how we design toward the "pluriverse."

Arturo: For me, transition design is the creative and somewhat organized dimension of the repair/crafting process that brings about a world from which heterogeneous futures can emerge. So far we are living in an awful, impoverished present. Transition design is the process by which we reorient—and hopefully transcend—mainstream, hetero-patriarchal, capitalist, colonial, racist civilizational designs—mostly encoded in what we call today neoliberal globalization—with its bleak destiny.

There is a very compelling idea in contemporary design theory that suggests that the crisis—the Anthropocene, if you will—is accompanied by a defuturing process. A fundamental book about design's complicity and history with defuturing is Tony Fry's *Defuturing: A New Design Philosophy* (1999, just republished in 2021). Fry charts all of the progressive changes that explain how we went from having many possible futures to the narrow futurity of today—and all within about a hundred years. From where we are standing, our future is defined by unimaginable suffering, ecological devastation, poverty, exploitation, and an immanent sense that the world's destiny is a massive extinction. Modern design has left us with this singular doomsday design.

The idea now is that a great deal of what design has to do is to reopen the possibility of different futures and futures in difference. This is what we call the futuring dimension of design. It is an ontological dimension of design practice—and precisely where the pluriverse comes into play.

The pluriverse refers to a world where many worlds fit. It's not just more possible futures within the same overarching conception of the world. There must always be—there are now—radically different conceptions of the world and, hence, multiple plausible futures. Heterogeneity is key.

This concept actually comes from the Zapatista indigenous movement in Chiapas, Mexico. The Zapatistas invite us to imagine a world where many worlds could fit, including their own indigenous world. They were the first to articulate this concept in contemporary politics. We may say, following their guide, that every encounter between worlds is an encounter between designs of different worlds. It's a phrase that reads much better in Spanish: *El encuentro entre mundos es el encuentro entre diseños de mundo*. This statement makes it clear that there was never an expectation that differently designed worlds couldn't or wouldn't meet. Instead, the Zapatistas advocate for symmetrical encounters while acknowledging that power differentials between diverse ways of worlding have to be controlled.

Marisa: I appreciate your use of the phrase "differently designed worlds," which succinctly communicates a multiplicity rooted in difference. Can you say more about this idea, which is at the heart of your notion of the pluriverse, and how it relates to transition design?

Arturo: So far I've come to six guidelines or axes for transitions, which I use as a tool to narrativize a notion of the pluriversal futures. I should clarify that this is what I see and hear as emerging from multiple struggles and experiments in Latin America (but possibly applicable to other regions of the world), not just something I am making up on my own.

The first principle is the recommunalization of social life. In the last two hundred years—and even more over the last fifty years of neoliberal globalization—communal forms of life have been fiercely attacked and marginalized. Generally speaking, each social group has to imagine what can best work for them in terms of reconstituting themselves as a community, with humans and other living beings. I like looking at projects like *Open Collectives*[2] to imagine how we might move in this direction.

The second criterion is the relocalization of productive and cultural activities to counteract the generalized delocalization that accompanies globalization. I see this as the natural continuation of the first criterion. We must do away with the structures that systematically erode our autonomy. Instead of making life with others, we end up outsourcing most of it to corporations, experts, and the state. Food production is perhaps one of the first fields that has benefited from this approach so far. It's being relocalized in antisystemic ways that generate a whole new set of practices around growing food, consuming food, and processing food. But we can't stop there. While not everything can be deglobalized, many activities can—in the domains of transportation, health, building, energy, and so forth.

The third criterion is the building and strengthening of local autonomies and direct democracy. Modernity has been five hundred years of progressive movement away from autonomous life production. Forget about states; forget about the United Nations; forget about The World Bank; forget about all these institutions that waste our labor, time, and intentions. They will never achieve the transition that is needed or that we are aiming for. Many groups and movements are now building from the ground up, and autonomy is the political dimension of these processes.

The fourth criterion is the simultaneous depatriarchization, deracialization, and decolonization of society. Patriarchy is a cosmovision and ontology that privileges control, hierarchies, appropriation, the negation of "the other" and, ultimately, violence and war. If we look around, every single violent society we see is a patriarchal society—this is how we end up with the Trump(s), the

Bolsonaro(s), and the Uribe(s) of the world.

The fifth point is the reintegration with the earth— or what indigenous groups in Colombia call the liberation of Mother Earth. As they argue, the earth has been enslaved, and as long as she's enslaved, so are we: humans and nonhumans alike. The thinking from radical interdependence clearly fits in here. There is a lot of thinking in this area in ecological design, biodesign, biophilic urbanism, and so forth; it needs to be pushed toward fulfilling the ontology of interdependence rather that remaining within an anthropocentric mindset with "nature" as exterior to us.

And, finally, the last criterion is the enhancement of the pluriverse. Like we've discussed, we need to fracture the single, globalized world—its discourse and practices—and reweave our doomsday design into one of heterogeneous futures. To do this, it's necessary to bring an end to global capital, global markets, and global consumption. This axis thus calls for fostering convergence among networks of place-based and regional transformative alternatives by creating horizontal, rhizomatic, self-organizing meshworks among them throughout countries and transnationally.

Rafi: Let's return to your concept of interdependence. What is the future of individualism in a postcapitalist context? How do we design our built environment in ways that counter entrenched notions of individualism and consumerism?

Arturo: The standard modern worldview is based on a hierarchical logic arising from the ontological premise of separation: humans are separate from nonhumans; individuals are separate from communities; reason is separate from emotion; mind is separate from body. This dualist ontology instills separation "all the way down," so to speak, in all we do and design. I think the image of *redes* embodies the continuity that this dualism excludes. When a net moves, a ripple moves through it all—every tear, movement, and repair is a realignment.

The future of individualism as imagined by the pluriverse is one where a particular brand of individualism is left behind—an individualism that substantiates hegemonic liberalism, private property, and representative democracy. It might be too early to anticipate what the legacy, remnants, and transformations of this individualism might be. Instead, we might speak of persons-in-relation; these relations include a range of human and nonhuman entities; among the latter, some groups in the Global South include spirits, ancestors, and even the wind, rivers, mountains, or stones.

That said, from my markedly Latin American perspective, when I think of how individualism is reified in the built environment, the images that comes to mind are those middle-class quarters, apartments, or houses designed for the nuclear family. According to that mindset, the larger the better. They frequent shopping centers—perhaps one of the most damaging urban social experiences—and they drive individually owned cars. This middle-class urban model is still offered as *the* model for all inhabitants of the city to follow. But as a way of living, it is radically decommunalized and delocalized, profoundly antiecological in its consumerist orientation, and a huge challenge for urban planning and design. Postdevelopment theory believes quite plainly that this model for life is unsustainable—and frankly undesirable. Perhaps certain appliances and technologies designed for this kind of home might endure, but I do see the need to question, and hopefully leave behind, this naturalized spatial model of middle-class living.

For my students, I often use the example of the *maloca* versus the typical suburban American home as a way to get them thinking about how particular designs—a *spatial* design, in this case—shape so much of who we are and what we do and to get them imagining alternatives. The *maloca* is a form of collective housing found among indigenous peoples in the Amazon. Similar structures exist in Papua New Guinea, and they existed as longhouses in some indigenous communities of North America. They are structures where thirty, forty, sometimes even fifty people live their daily lives without separation. Naturally, there are understood rules for behavior and structuring life, but ultimately the form of life that emerges is one that produces communal forms of life, resulting in profound interconnection and relationality with all living beings. At the other end of the spectrum, there is the typical suburban house—a structure celebrated by 1950s Hollywood in a very patriarchal moment in American history. These homes are emblematic of hetero-patriarchal family life rooted in consumption—ideally, they have car garages, dishwashers, tall hedges, and many walls. The kind of life that emerges here is nonrelational: the life of the individual. The people who live in suburban homes are conditioned to aspire to ownership and thus become entrenched in markets that require professionalization. This is a clear illustration of the simple formula that Anne-Marie Willis, an Australian design theorist, coined about twenty years ago: "Design designs."

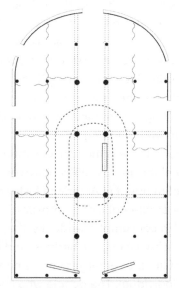

Top: Photo of Maloca of the Cuduiari river that flows between Brazil and Colombia, painted with colorful motifs. Koch-Grünberg, 1904.

Bottom: Floor plan of a typical Maloca. Floor plan drawn by authors based on S. Hugh-Jones, 1985.

Marisa: Why is transition design particularly urgent today?

Arturo: It depends where you are looking. The field of transition design has been under development in the United States for over ten years, led by a small group at Carnegie Mellon's School of Design. In the Global South, transition design is just beginning to be discussed today, and I would say that there it has a more explicitly political approach. In Latin America, it really is impossible to suggest any transition without speaking about capitalism and inequality from the start—almost to the point where it is taken for granted. In Colombia, inequality is jarring: 1 percent of the population owns 80 percent of Colombia's agricultural land, leaving 20 percent of the land to be distributed among the other 99 percent. It's not an unusual statistic for Latin America.

Meanwhile, as a professor and academic in the United States, I've found it almost impossible to articulate a critique of capitalism. In the United States, there are even feminist groups and antiracist groups that don't have a substantial critique of capitalism. Clearly, this is not because inequality doesn't affect the United States. Worldwide, the wealthiest 1 percent control 50 percent of global wealth. Still, in the United States, critiques of capitalism are considered a dead end politically. In Latin America, it's quite literally just the beginning. That's where you start, and then you move on to how we can think of noncapitalist, postcapitalist, nonliberal, or postliberal social configurations.

Capitalism claims individual autonomy and the myth of the self-sufficient individual by invisibilizing the vertical structures of oppression and domination that keep the myth alive. This is why proponents of the commons and commoning such as David Bollier and Silke Helfrich call for a veritable "OntoShift"—a shift to a different story of life from that of the possessive and competitive individual—if we are to undermine the naturalized ideologies of capitalism. The stigma against the commons emerges because we are not able to imagine how to organize social and economic life more collectively and horizontally. The idea is not that everything is going to become a commons but that these spaces of the commons are going to become more ubiquitous as they connect with each other. Think of *redes*: in this kind of constellation, these common territories can (ideally) make an effective dent in global capitalism. Commoning advocate David Bollier summarized well this state of affairs in a recent interview: "Emergence happens. . . . Rather than proposing a glowing vision of a commons-based society, I am content to point to hundreds of smaller-scale projects and movements. As they find each other, replicate their innovations, and federate into a more coordinated, self-aware polity—if we dare call it that!—well, that's when things will get very interesting."[3]

From where we are standing, it is clear that our *redes* are ruptured. The global crisis and the Covid pandemic have proven that the bankers, the economists, the engineers, and the corporate elite are not the ones who care about us and the earth. Nurses, caregivers, mothers, migrants, and indigenous stewards of the environment have always been at the center of care. Transition design and autonomous design need to embrace a *feminine strategy*—encompassing caring, healing, mending, *tejido* making, and commoning, among other actions. This is why I have come to define design as a praxis for the healing of and caring for the web of life, and we are all invited to take part in that.

Notes

1. Gilles Deleuze and Félix Guattari, *A Thousand Plateaus* (Minneapolis: University of Minnesota Press, 1987).
2. *Open Collectives* is an exhibit at the 17th International Venice Biennale of Architecture. It was led by MIT associate professors Rafi Segal (architecture) and Sarah Williams (civic data design) with collaborators Marisa Morán Jahn and Greg Lindsay.
3. "The Future Is a 'Pluriverse': An Interview with David Bollier," Grassroots Economic Organizing, May 22, 2017, https://geo.coop/story/future-pluriverse. See also David Bollier and Silke Helfrich's excellent and very design-friendly book, *Free, Fair and Alive* (Gabriola Island, BC: New Society, 2019).

On Solidarity and Political Emancipation

Jessica Gordon Nembhard

Vectors of Liberation

Rafi: Thanks for talking with us, Jessica. To give you a bit of context about where we intersect, I come from Israel, where I grew up visiting my grandparents who lived on a kibbutz. This experience and all its complexities has informed my work as an architect: I'm interested in the role that *physical spaces* have in shaping and strengthening collectives. In other words, how can architecture and design give form to collectives?

> **Marisa:** And Jessica, my path toward your work comes in part from the intersection between movement building and art. A big part of my work since 2010 is in collaboratively producing public art and creative media with domestic workers. For those of us involved in the movement for domestic workers' rights, strategies of in/visibility are paramount, since for so long domestic work has been made intentionally invisible by those in power. As an artist, one of my roles is to make the legacy and labor of care visible.
>
> What I find fascinating about your scholarship on the Black economic solidarity movement is that it has often had to remain *hidden* from view—and necessarily so. What do these spaces of refuge, mutual support, and emancipation look like, and what would it mean to make them visible?

Rafi: So one of the things we wanted to ask you about, Jessica, is the spatial aspect of the Underground Railroad.

Jessica: First, we cannot discount how land and spaces of liberation form a central experience in enslavement. As a slave, you were separated from your body and from the ownership of any land or assets. So every action to reaffirm humanity and reclaim social or economic life required taking back some kind of space. This space can be as little as the plot of land adjacent to slave cabins where a group of people could plant some food. In other words, *nutrition requires space*. But you also needed that plot of land in order to control your food supply so that you could augment what you needed to escape from enslavement. So here *space is linked to independence and liberation.*

We also might think of the body as a kind of space, moving across political boundaries into a space where you regained bodily sovereignty and political emancipation.

Marisa: Interesting. So spatially one aspect of the Underground Railroad is as a *vector* created by people pooling together resources and knowledge . . .

Jessica: Yes, the Underground Railroad itself was a solidarity system that consisted of vehicles like wagons, trails crossing territories, and houses with hidden basements that only family members knew how to access. In most of these cases, the landowners or wagon owners were white allies who had more rights and resources—but like Black communities, they still had to disguise how they were using the space. Blacks provided less-tangible assets for the Underground Railroad such as planning and leadership. They were

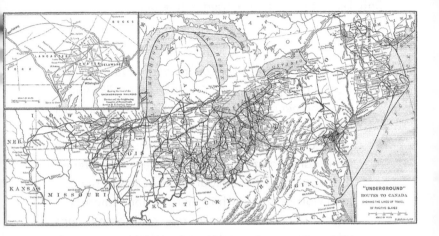

Underground Railroad routes to Canada, showing the lines of travel of fugitive slaves.

W. H. Siegel, 1898. Library of Congress with lines re-emphasized by authors.

organizers and guides as well as the passengers. All this had to be done in secret and strategically.

Rafi: Can you talk about how physical 'brick and mortar' spaces were disguised?"

Jessica: Buildings and public spaces appeared to have a certain function, but they could also be used for something else. Churches, for example, played an important role in politicizing Black communities toward collectivization. If you followed all the rules of what a church would look like from the outside, you were given some level of autonomy: the churches and religious gatherings provided a "cover" for other things. While you were talking to people about religion, you could also be talking about other things without drawing attention to what you were doing.

Rafi: Did the necessarily closed nature of the organizations contribute a sense of commitment or solidarity?

> **Jessica:** Absolutely! For co-ops and mutual aid groups, trust is really important. You have to feel like you trust the people that you're working with. This trust made it possible for economic enterprises such as credit unions to form. Churches function as important fraternal organizations that nurture camaraderie; they have a built-in solidarity because you're not then worried about who's there or not. Fraternal organizations play a similar role, and some groups rely upon bonding and trust-building training and ceremonies.

Rafi: What are some of the other factors that enabled Black mutual aid societies to flourish?

> **Jessica:** Well, pooling all kinds of resources and access to capital are important. The sources of financial equity can range from members' investment, to bank or credit union lending, to worker-owners putting in sweat equity, to government grants.

Marisa: Can you say more about the importance to members of co-ops? How did the equity they provided compare to other sources of revenue?

> **Jessica:** What's important to know is that you don't have to be middle class to join or start a co-op. With worker co-ops, you can pay annual dues or buy equity shares in installments from the wage that you earn in the co-op. The whole point is that you don't have to come to the co-op with money because you can earn it as you work. Other Black co-ops also allowed their members to pay in installments so that

they could afford to be a member. It's also important to note that the mainstream co-op movement then and now doesn't have as many examples of low-income co-ops—but they are really important as an antipoverty strategy.

On the other hand, there are a number of examples of co-ops whose strength and longevity are attributed to Black middle-class members whose steady jobs meant they could contribute more equity and with more consistency. When you look through history, the groups that had economically stable members definitely helped self-finance a co-op's early years—especially in the 1800s and 1900s, when there weren't other sources of revenue or loans. There were many examples of low-income co-ops as well, so middle-class status is not the only way to address the financial need.

Rafi: What about government support? What role has the government played in supporting co-ops? What role could they play?

Jessica: The government could be playing a stronger role today to support co-ops! Consider this: today we have different kinds of state and federal support for low-income people in the form of vouchers, subsidies, or cash support. But we *should be* thinking about public money as belonging to us. We *should be* able to put it toward supporting co-ops and solidarity economy endeavors among low-income people especially.

For example, in the 1930s and 1940s, the New Deal had a self-help co-op division in the Department of Commerce that would actually give money to unemployed people to help them start co-ops. Also some municipalities put money into helping people convert their apartment buildings into limited equity housing co-ops.

We could also think of reparations money as a way to help people develop co-ops—to support both nonextractive co-op loan funds and education and training in cooperative economics.

Just because people don't have money themselves doesn't mean they don't deserve or can't participate in a co-op. In some ways, we don't have the money or the assets because we've been stripped of our assets through racial capitalism. We've been denied access to capital through years of apartheid and economic discrimination. So in lots of ways, the fact that we don't have that initial capital to put into a co-op is a function of structural racism. Therefore, we should think about public money as belonging to us to address structural inequalities.

Co-ops, Crises, Movements

Rafi: You've written about how people turn to co-ops and mutual aid societies during times of recession. As we teeter into a recession, what takeaways can inform the socioeconomic resilience of communities—especially historically underserved communities—today?

Jessica: Crises are when co-ops shine. Those of us who study co-ops notice that a lot more co-ops get created during times of crisis and enable communities to survive those crises. The Great Depression in the 1930s was the period I found with the most active cooperative development among African American communities. And these co-ops in turn enabled other Black organizations to flourish. Then, during the Great Recession of 2007–2010, we also saw more people looking for alternatives and starting co-ops. And since the Covid pandemic, mutual aid has proliferated.

Now, people are more convinced that we can't just patch up—we have to make change and think outside the box. And today we have organizations interested in and willing and able to keep the mutual aid and co-op movements going along with international support, which always helps.

Marisa: Let's talk about movements. We're talking to you at a moment of social unrest, when America is reckoning with its history of racial divides. Can you talk about the relationship between Black economic solidarity and Black Lives Matter?

Jessica: Struggles against police brutality, a police state, and the Black Lives Matters movement are founded on a platform of economic justice. To achieve this, we need to fight for collective ownership and group economic solutions to our housing, food, and labor problems and for all aspects of state violence and institutional racism. We need to make structures that are nonexploitative. In the 1960s, the Black Panthers emphasized the importance of economic justice. They weren't just reacting to something; they were trying to build spaces, activities, connections for the long run for the largest number of people over time—and that includes our own self-determination and solidarity as a group process. This process continues today with the Movement for Black Lives' platform on economic justice through solidarity and cooperative economics.

Marisa: Can you talk about the role of cooperatives in strengthening women's economic and political power?

Jessica: In my research, this was one of the fascinating findings: over and over again throughout history, co-ops have thrived when women were centrally involved as founders, leaders, managers, and workers. Once I started looking at it, women were central to the co-ops as much as the co-ops were central to the women. Women's leadership made co-ops successful, and their involvement is what helped them be successful outside of co-ops. And in fact, the importance of black women's social energy and skills in co-ops was always recognized by black men.

In particular, the black co-op movement really needed and relied upon women's energy. Those founded by black women were the strongest. By the time you got to the mid-1800s, most mutual aid societies—even the mainstream ones—were either run by or founded by black women, and then the same was true with co-ops by the twentieth century. In one example, the African American civil rights activist, educator, and religious leader Nannie Helen Boroughs, from Washington, DC, was thanked by the National Cooperative Business Association for her work in the co-op movement.

Baltimore, Self-Education, and Long-Term Impact

Rafi: Marisa and I, together with a third partner, an urban planner and developer named Ernst Valery, are collaborating on what we are calling Carehaus—it's a multigenerational coliving project in Baltimore, where caregivers and older people live together. Carehaus is directly influenced by co-op models and Baltimore's fascinating history.

Jessica: Ah, Baltimore! A city with a truly interesting history of black mutualistic societies!

Rafi: Exactly! We are wondering if you can talk about this a bit.

Jessica: There are many fascinating examples of early cooperation within the black community in Baltimore, starting from the seventeenth century. In his book about economic cooperation published in 1895 and his book about co-ops published in 1907, W. E. B. Du Bois notes that Baltimore had the most mutual aid societies and co-ops.

One of the things that made Baltimore's co-ops relatively unique was that they were comprised of both middle-class and working-class blacks supporting each other. Baltimore had a thriving black skilled workforce.

At the end of the Civil War, Maryland was a union state but still a slave state. Maryland only ended slavery three years after the Emancipation Proclamation when the Thirteenth Amendment was ratified on December 6, 1865. During this time, only whites were allowed to own businesses.

Baltimore is a port city. Its economy thrives on shipping. The black caulkers and stevedores (the people who loaded and unloaded ships) were considered the most talented and highly trained. Whites neither wanted to nor could compete with that workforce, and they tried to ban black caulkers and stevedores from working independently. So blacks in Baltimore combined efforts to create a multiracial co-op–like organization called the Chesapeake Marine Railway and Dry Dock Company that lasted eighteen years. One of the things enabling Chesapeake Dry Dock to survive for so long was that it was backed by black co-ops and credit unions and by middle-class Blacks who joined as equal members, or shareholders. So this ability to work across economic divides shows you how close the black community was in Baltimore.

By the time Chesapeake Dry Dock disbanded in 1883, all two hundred workers joined other shipyards and unions. This is a success because it shows you how the education and skills that you build in co-ops build toward long-term economic advancement for the workers and their families—and it would not have happened without the special configuration and mission of the Chesapeake Marine Railway and Dry Dock Company. So in addition to solving immediate challenges of access and employment, co-ops and mutual aid societies also provide essential education and training that workers and members carry with them—even after the co-op disbands.

Marisa: Building on that, one of the ways we see Carehaus is as an architectural project, yes, but also as an economic project that provides workforce training and financial literacy. Can you talk about the importance of self-study in the lifespan of mutual aid groups and co-ops?

Jessica: Historically, the strongest co-ops also start with an intentional study group, which then becomes sustained training and education throughout the lifespan of the organization. The educational component of black co-ops was a key component of maintaining the members' commitment to do everything to get a project off the ground. This human sense of commitment to the project matters. Some co-ops today even pay people to attend meetings and trainings because education is so central to co-ops. Those that skimped on the educational piece all floundered.

There are times in history when education about co-ops was more widely accessible and known. Today this is missing. We need to get the word out and make people more confident about co-ops as viable and strong economic alternatives.

And it's important to point out that even among those co-ops that don't necessarily last long, if they have strong social energy, they have an important lasting effect.

Rafi: Can you say more about the impact, or effect, of mutual aid societies and co-ops?

Jessica: Because Black Americans were discriminated against, the only way we could survive was by pooling resources and leveraging how we work together. In some ways, people did it for their families to feed them and to get places to live. In some ways, it was individualistic. But because racial capitalism doesn't allow you to make it without working with other people, you really ended up with two major accomplishments. First, working together enabled us to obtain food to eat and places to live, build assets, hone skills, buy land, and save money. This foundation then becomes a critical stepping-stone for some of us into the capitalist system.

But that mutualistic support and interdependence are carried forward. You can't exist in collectives without recognizing how others in the group are also prospering. People saw that collective action is what made them strong. So our personal liberation has always been tied to collective emancipation.

That's why I love this history of co-ops—because the process of solidarity doesn't really leave you. And as a group, Black Americans have used solidarity and cooperative economics not just to survive but for group liberation.

On Labor and Cooperatives

Trebor Scholz

Platform Cooperatives

Rafi: Let's lay a foundation. What are platform cooperatives, and what are their main tenets?

> **Trebor:** Those among us in this field share these tenets: platform cooperatives are based on the broad-based ownership of platforms. This includes also users and not only workers. Platform cooperatives also function through democratic governance.
>
> However, I believe open-source design and inclusive design are important characteristics. The hope is not to go with a traditional Silicon Valley design of software but to really design platforms in participation with the communities they are meant to serve. It's actually very hard to communicate the importance of open-source design; I can't overstate this. A lot of efforts are replicated in an infuriating way across the global ecosystem, where people spend millions of dollars on the exact same project. However, we don't seem to be willing to open up these processes.

Marisa: What's your definition of a cooperative? And how does it differ from a collective?

> **Trebor:** Cooperatives are a very defined way of organizing businesses. They are voluntary

organizations. In 1844, the Rochdale Society of Equitable Pioneers agreed to seven central tenets that were later updated in 1966. Called the Rochdale Principles, they are

1. Open membership
2. Democratic control
3. Dividend on purchase
4. Limited interest on capital
5. Political and religious neutrality
6. Cash trading
7. Promotion of education

Co-ops—and platform co-ops—are different from social enterprises. Not that they aren't aligned. The B Corp movement is a step in the right direction, but I think that platform co-ops are more radical. The big differentiator is ownership. If the workers and the people who depend on this platform don't own it, you can't really have substantial change.

And I believe you can't really have substantive change without organizational ownership. There are various advocacy groups that have tried to introduce a score for noncooperative digital platforms that grades how well you treat your workers. I think it's a wonderful idea in social democracies. Perhaps it will work fantastically well in Germany, maybe Sweden, or Denmark. But I can also assure you that Amazon and these big companies couldn't care less. They couldn't care less about the score they get. They get such terrible reviews every day in the news, and clearly the public's opinion isn't really swayed. You can't shame them! Public campaigns are great and necessary and a good thing to do. But we have years and years of terrible press about Uber. And the negative reviews

PHOTOGRAPH OF THIRTEEN OF THE ORIGINAL MEMBERS
OF THE
ROCHDALE EQUITABLE PIONEERS' SOCIETY.

1. JAMES STANDRING.   2. JOHN BENT.   3. JAMES SMITHIES.   4. CHARLES HOWARTH.   5. DAVID BROOKS.   6. BENJ. RUDMAN.   7. JOHN SCOWCROFT.
8. JAMES MANOCK.   9. JOHN COLLIER.   10. SAMUEL ASHWORTH.   11. WILLIAM COOPER.   12. JAMES TWEEDALE.   13. JOSEPH SMITH.

Founded in Manchester, England in 1844, the original Rochdale Society of Equitable Pioneers established the basis of co-ops as we know them today. Charles Heyworth, seated behind the desk, was a warper in the flannel industry who helped start various co-ops. Heyworth successfully advocated for the ten-hour work day and other progressive labor standards of the time. Charles Heyworth, one of the original Rochdale Pioneers who envisioned the central tenets of cooperatives still operative today, was honored in a commemorative stamp by the Venezuelan government during the 1944 Centenary of the foundation of the cooperative of Rochdale. Unknown photographer, Library of Congress, circa 1844 and 1846.

don't seem to matter! You have to really never ever touch a newspaper to not understand that the drivers are totally exploited. And yet people seem to accept this. I have my doubts about how substantive change can be brought about unless you own the structure yourself and make those changes through your own control.

Marisa: Can you say more about how the financial (fiduciary) differences of cooperatives and for-profit businesses shape our social fabric? In other words, how does the experience of being a worker in a co-op feel different from the experience of working for a venture capitalist business?

Trebor: I think about this through the example of Airbnb. Friends of mine worked with them—and they are wonderful human beings. That has nothing to do with this. All your humanity has nothing to do with the inevitable logic of the venture capital model.

The venture capitalist model requires you by charter to suck out the value of communities because that is what the very heart of that model is. You have to extract data. You have to extract value from those communities.

It's also not about building businesses, right? When you look at Silicon Valley, it's really largely aiming for selling your business to Google or Apple or Facebook— becoming significant enough as a threat to be taken over. It's not really about the people that are served by these organizations. It's really about becoming rich.

But in life, we have the choice to not become a vacuum cleaner that sucks out the money and resources from communities. There are alternatives! And this is where I think the cooperative model is very different. Because it follows an entirely different logic. It's actually about the people who depend on this the most—the people who depend on this platform to work. But it's also the users. I think this is a really significant and inescapable difference.

So, for example, you have many platform co-ops like Loconomics in San Francisco. In their bylaws, they basically make it impossible for the platform co-op to be sold. They cannot be sold to Facebook, even if there is a very attractive offer on the table. They even put this into the Loconomics bylaws. Because they don't even trust themselves, they decided to put outside people in place so that if it comes to it, the outside people could overturn the people who started the cooperative. If a billion-dollar offer comes, they will have to say no.

Marisa: What are the competitive advantages of cooperatives?

Trebor: There are many! Cooperatives create high-quality jobs. Cooperatives are 5 percent more productive on average than employee-owned companies. They are more resilient than other business forms—we saw that after 2008. After the first five years of operation, they are more resilient than other businesses. Cooperatives have lower worker turnover. There's less absenteeism among the workers. There's more control over privacy and transparency. Cooperatives ensure fair pay and also the opportunity to benefit a whole ecosystem of cooperatives, which is something you don't have with corporations. Further, cooperatives allow for greater control—in particular, through governance of the direction where the business goes.

These are the points that are always brought up. But there's something else that I want to mention. I saw this in South Africa when I visited a sewing cooperative of six women. I really saw the advantages of their cooperative and the really heartfelt experiences of the workers. The cooperative really meant an enormous amount to people's lives. One woman I spoke with emphasized that usually the alternative would be to work in a factory. In a factory, she would have a singular boss who would not necessarily let her leave early, even if she was sick. So the dignity-at-work aspect is very important. It's significant when six women are their own boss in a cooperative.

So these slogans about governance and democracy are all very abstract, but if you actually meet the people, you see this really uplifting experience. There's nothing abstract about that.

Rafi: Do co-ops tend to lean one way or the other in terms of political tendencies?

Trebor: Co-ops are definitely not ideological. And co-ops are by no means necessarily leftist at all. This has become clear to me after talking with cooperatives in Brazil about the right-wing president Jair Bolsonaro or even the many agricultural cooperatives in the middle of the United States who vote conservatively.

Unionized worker cooperatives, however, are deeply progressive communities. In the United States, there are very few examples of unionized worker cooperatives—I think there are roughly only around four hundred. But in France, you have seven hundred thousand! And in Italy, 30 percent of the economy consists of unionized worker cooperatives. That's one of the real differences between the United States and other countries: a recognition of the power of collectivity—that if you work together, you can actually create a better life for yourself.

If you look at 1844 Rochdale, New Manchester— where cooperatives started—it's basically the area where unions started at the same time. And both emerged from the same impetus: helping workers. Nobody cared if you called them a co-op or a union;

they were basically the same thing. The only question was, How will we make the life of these deeply miserable people better? I think this is essential to remember today when cooperatives and unions are artificially pitted against each other in competition.

Measuring Impact

Marisa: Here in the United States, people conflate the success of a business with its scale, reach, or longevity. But co-ops have a different way of measuring impact. Could you elaborate?

> **Trebor:** Progressives—the traditional Left—always get hung up around the idea of scale, which they conflate with success. They say, "What a great idea, but it doesn't scale." If it's not destroying Uber, it therefore has no right to exist. However, from research, you see that cooperatives historically coexist with corporations. They don't replace them.
>
> When it comes to scaling, I think there is a lot of Silicon Valley ideology seeping into people's thinking about these things. Still, there are economically successful platform co-ops, like Stocksy in Canada, which has around eleven hundred photographers from sixty to seventy countries. It's a global cooperative that made $13 million last year. I would call it successful. I think they have fifty-five employees.
>
> But in general, if a project doesn't achieve global domination, people think, What good is it? But why can't a domestic worker cooperative like Up-and-Go in New York City have a platform that works just fine in the city? I would certainly consider it a success. Most labor-oriented cooperatives usually tend to be small with no ambition to take over the planet.

The idea of one monopoly is a very Silicon Valley idea. Why not replicate the software in another town and have the workers there determine how they want to run their organization? That's exactly what people are doing. Actually, here in New York City, Brightly Cleaning Cooperative just created a franchise model for cooperatives that allows the formation of cleaning cooperatives that could then eventually join the platform co-op. The platform becomes an umbrella for all these smaller cooperatives. I think of *replication* as a way of scaling.

Still, I think there are some sectors where you do have to have one platform—for example, in transportation. It's just extremely expensive to rival something like Uber. I worked with transportation cooperatives in Brazil, and they tried to generate an alternate model, but it's very expensive. I think in this case transportation cooperatives will need international leadership and organization to facilitate the production of an international transportation platform that will then serve cooperatives all over the world. And the same goes for short-term housing rentals. I think these are the two areas where this local model doesn't work.

Strengthening Co-ops

Rafi: What can governments do to strengthen cooperatives? What kinds of support and policies could strengthen cooperatives?

Trebor: Traditionally, Democrats in the United States faithfully believe that *regulation* will take care of a lot of the problems that workers in the United States now face. Other countries around the world like Italy also share this same faith in government regulation. Look at India, right? With Modi. And look at China, right? Hong Kong. These conflicts suggest that their governments are not playing the role that they ought to play when it comes to the protection of workers. So whether or not the federal government can act as a vehicle of regulation that benefits workers is in question.

On a smaller municipal scale, co-ops can function as a bit of a shield for workers in a system that seems to be falling apart. I think that this is why co-ops are taken much more seriously now than they were even five or six years ago. People are starting to see co-ops as something to resort to. They are not the ultimate solution to anything, but they can offer temporary protection for workers.

The question of how policy makers can support this work is not that difficult to answer. There are quite clear obstacles. In the United States, for example, it's cartel law. Smaller cooperatives agreeing to sell their services through a platform can very easily be interpreted as price-fixing—but only if it has the scale to become significant enough to lawmakers—which, of course, would be hilarious and horrendous. Look at what corporations are doing! But there needs to be an exception for cooperatives. I think there's a union exception already in American law, and there should be one for platform co-ops as well. Many people are already taking on cooperatives, especially platform cooperatives. Senator Gillibrand in the United States has been supportive.

But here's a good policy opportunity: in Germany and other European countries, venture capitalist–funded start-ups receive quite massive tax advantages. But if you do the exact same thing as a cooperative, you don't get those advantages. So that's, of course, a problem. As a society, we should be thinking about how to achieve parity for platform cooperatives.

Marisa: What places have created policies that enable co-ops to thrive?

> **Trebor:** I was amazed to see that in Kerala, a socialist state in the south of India, has committed itself to building an ecosystem of platform cooperatives. They started with five hundred thousand taxi drivers in January 2020. And will now likely size up. It's highly encouraging. See? On a state level, they are willing to change the laws to make this happen.
>
> Of course, they have the power of the state to actually implement these changes—so they can just tell cab drivers what to do. This brings its own problems, but it's also advantageous.

Digital Economy and Labor Exploitation

Rafi: Why are cooperatives important in today's gig economy?

> **Trebor:** There are many different reasons that cooperatives are more relevant today—perhaps even more relevant than ten years ago. Unionized worker cooperatives can play really critical roles in redressing the labor exploitation or price gouging we see rampant in the Ubers, Airbnbs, and Lyfts of today.
>
> I mean it's really fascinating. When you look at studies on the gig economy, it's very hard to substantively learn about the gig economy. All the companies say, "It's all a trade secret." They refuse to share anything about how many workers they have or who they are.

A gig economy research lab at Cornell University found that one of the largest problems faced by gig workers is harassment—racial harassment, sexual harassment, etc. Salaried workers protected under the 1938 Fair Labor Standards Act would have legal recourse, but these same laws don't protect freelancers and gig workers.

If you look at staggering economic inequality, it is not a surprise that worker cooperatives in the United States are 65 percent women of color. This is also a sign that worker cooperatives are really helping and supporting the most precarious workers.

Marisa: How do platform cooperatives address worker precarity, and what are the pitfalls to watch out for?

Trebor: I don't have an idealized view of cooperatives. Many of them are misogynist. It's often older white men in power. They have a real problem in terms of getting young people involved. There are many negative experiences that all young people's parents had with cooperatives that taint their perspectives: self-exploitation, government control, etc. So I think there are many possibilities for this to fail.

However, I think what's exciting is that millennials are quite enthusiastic about platform co-ops because they see this as a reinvigoration of the cooperative model. What's important to note is that many countries do not legally allow or recognize cooperatives. In Brazil, for example, there's a co-op law from 1994 that literally describes what a co-op is allowed to do and turns out to be extremely restrictive. In Japan, worker co-ops are not even part of the law. In Indonesia, they haven't even heard of worker co-ops. So around the world, education about co-ops and platform cooperatives is really urgent. Today's digital platforms can help share this information more widely.

Going back to the Rochdale Principles, one tenet is that cooperatives help other cooperatives. In the digital age, this could look like data sharing. There's a home-care cooperative in Britain that is launching as a traditional sort of digital start-up, but it is funded through community-funded crowd equity instead of a venture capital model. In Britain, they are lucky because there's a tax model that incentivizes this way of raising money. Because of this, the cooperative movement in the UK actually raised £112 million through a community shares model. So data sharing among co-ops is a competitive advantage over venture capitalist start-ups or for-profit companies, which usually closely guard their data.

In addition, because co-ops can control the governance of the platform, this can be a real competitive advantage: you can decide how much privacy you grant your workers and how much privacy you grant your users.

Governance, Civic Agency

Rafi: Some co-ops are six people; some are in the hundreds of thousands. Could you explain how we might begin to understand democratic governance models for cooperatives of different sizes? In other words, can these two conditions of communal ownership and democratic governance operate on multiple scales?

Trebor: People around the world forming cooperatives always face the same problem—governance. People often think that technology is the burning problem. But it turns out that it's definitely not the *main* problem. The main problem is that people can't get along. They can't decide on anything. They can't even decide on higher wages because some people say they want more free time. The challenge is to get people to set common goals, to agree, and to decide jointly. It's very complicated.

This is really an opportunity for cooperatives organized around digital platforms because it can bring together geographically dispersed workers, give them a dignified livelihood, and engage them in questions about governance. We have various examples of platform cooperatives that are digitally organizing to strengthen the solidarity of freelancers all over the state of New York or Gujarat, India. Given the sudden, massive decline of industrial unions (which have been largely incapable of taking on the gig economy), there are some amazing experiments in the UK, for example, where people really think about innovative forms of unions. This is where these platforms can come in as a way of facilitating deliberation and decision-making.

Pandemic

Marisa: If in times of crises people come together in new ways to share resources, what have you seen during the Covid pandemic and its economic vagaries? Have you noticed new trends in terms of platform cooperatives and mutualistic enterprises?

Trebor: One of the main trends we've seen is that people are turning to each other for support, especially as government safety nets collapse.

We've seen a new dynamism of interest in platform cooperatives, a greater willingness and understanding to embrace co-op models in response to the pandemic, even on behalf of more traditional institutions, which in prepandemic time were slower and more difficult to engage.

The interest in platform cooperative teach-ins also grew exponentially. Working relationships we had previously established with forty-seven organizations from around the world experienced a boost in eagerness and urgency to "get to work"—leading in many cases to launching platform cooperative incubators across the world.

Rafi: Can you give a few examples? And what takeaways can you share?

Trebor: Many co-ops emerged in response to the pandemic; some were temporary, but others continue to exist. The state of Kerala in southern India, for example, wrote platform cooperatives into their five-year policy plan and have now set the goal of establishing thousands of platform co-ops!

In New York City, we saw the rise of a four-thousand-driver co-op rideshare platform as an alternative to Uber and Lyft. They have recently raised $1.5 million, which is not intended to be invested in the technology or the software, as in other gig economy start-ups, but rather in the cooperative itself. Interestingly, this co-op is run by a former Uber executive but in a completely different way. This example reminded us that in platform cooperatives, the investment is first of all in the people and social structure that establish the co-op.

In Bologna, Italy, for example, in response to the pandemic's recurring lockdowns and quarantines, we've witnessed an incredible co-op, a bike delivery system whereby young people redistribute goods to senior residents. Food that sat unused in restaurants, books that were locked up in public libraries, and more were being distributed—and in some cases even included around a twenty-minute daily conversation between the bike riders and the seniors. This platform was set up independently but was supported by data collected by the city.

What we have learned here is that platform cooperatives can be a way for city government to help residents be more resilient. Unlike historical examples of socialist countries where co-ops were established by the government, in the case of the Bologna the city government did not implement this co-op but merely created the conditions for it to be established. Through analyzing and sharing data about what residents needed most during the pandemic, the conditions were created for people to come together and self-organize.

Platform cooperatives seek, on the one hand, to break away from the gig economy as a product of Silicon Valley sharing start-ups and, on the other, to avoid the socialist/communist top-down practices of government-initiated co-ops. We are encouraged that there is a third way, where institutions and cities can take a role in encouraging and legally enabling residents to come together—in creating the right conditions for platform cooperatives to emerge. In places like Finland and New Zealand, for example, legislation is already more open to support such structures, and there is a more positive grassroot atmosphere. Perhaps this is beginning to happen in some places in the United States.

Change

Marisa: Can you talk about the relationship between cooperatives and social change?

> **Trebor:** One of the functions of co-ops is that they provide a stepping-stone perhaps to a postcapitalist future. They are not the revolution, nor are they capable of bringing down capitalism. Co-ops function firmly within capitalism, but they create conditions that can show us what a postcapitalist world could look like.
>
> For example, a venture capital–funded food-delivery start-up in Belgium failed but then became a cooperative when the couriers took over the start-up and the attending customers. This is a great example because the venture capital generated all these customers, and now this cooperative has gained the benefits.
>
> I think about cooperatives as a tool. One tool can't build alone; you need a *set* of tools to build something, right?

Rafi: Would you argue that we don't need a revolution if we have platform cooperatives?

> **Trebor:** No, I would not say that we don't need a revolution. Of course, we need a revolution. But from where I stand, I think we are too far away from a revolution. I think a lot of people had fantastic ideas about universal basic income or a postcapitalist society. If I look at all this kind of literature, I'm on board with most of it. But, realistically, this is not going to happen in most people's lifetime—and certainly not in my lifetime.
>
> I always think of Emma Goldman. She gave a fiery speech about the revolution, and there was an older

worker sitting in the front row who said, "What about me? I'm not going to experience a revolution." And it gave Goldman pause.

We saw that with Occupy Wall Street. And we've seen that with other movements as well. As positive of a role as they played, what was lacking was a concrete near-term alternative. I think this is what is so hopeful about cooperatives and so useful. And, yes, they are definitely flawed. Many co-ops are misogynist. Many are top-down. There are people in many countries like South Africa—or in fact all the socialist republics across Africa—who do not necessarily have positive associations with cooperatives because they are implemented by the state. These cooperatives were not grassroots projects. However, as a form, I think the unionized worker cooperative can really intervene positively, no matter the mixed history of cooperatives.

Designing for Co-ops and Mutualism

Marisa: Could you share with us some thoughts on the benefits that cooperatives might gain from collaborating with designers or architects?

> **Trebor:** Oh, how interesting—you're asking how platform co-ops can benefit from working with designers and urbanists and architects. There is, of course, a very physical aspect to all of this.
>
> There is a recipe to how cooperatives launch. They always involve legal scholars, legal professionals (usually legal scholars), policy makers such as mayors or people from the government, and, of course, technologists. A few platform cooperatives that recently started in Sweden, India, and other countries

always emerged in conversation with designers. But we haven't really thought about bringing urban planners to the table, which seems like something to consider as well.

Rafi: Well, we will just have to keep conversing and find ways to work together!

On Mutual Aid Societies and Digital-First Organizing

Greg Lindsay

As the Covid pandemic swept the world in the winter of 2020, thousands of local mutual aid groups spontaneously emerged to deliver food and critical supplies to isolated neighbors during the first wave of lockdowns. Coined by the anarchist philosopher Peter Kropotkin more than a century ago, *mutual aid* eschews charity for solidarity, relies on horizontal organizing rather than vertical leadership, and favors replicability over scalability. Notable historical examples include the Black Panther Party's free breakfast campaign, which at its peak in 1969 fed twenty thousand American children daily across thirty-six chapters—more free meals than provided by the state of California's program at the time.

More recently, mutual aid has come to be associated with bottom-up disaster relief in lieu or even in spite of official recovery efforts, including Hurricane Katrina's Common Ground Relief and Hurricane Sandy's Occupy Sandy, which comprised as many as sixty thousand volunteers. In this respect, the simultaneous flowering of mutual aid groups as a response to the virus might be expected. But they differ from their predecessors in two important ways.

While the pandemic is global in scope (albeit temporally and spatially uneven), contagion and quarantines have conspired to create innumerable "local" disasters—a situation without recent precedent. This required these new networks to be digital-first by necessity, relying on tools ranging in complexity from telephone numbers to Google docs, Slack channels, and Airtable spreadsheets. These free applications were essential to the overnight organization of new groups but also raise questions about their long-term structure, sustainability, and equity.

Once the pandemic ends, how will these networks and open collectives strive to harness both face-to-face organizing and digital tools? Will they be more persistent than their predecessors? And how are they evolving to face new crises? What follows are conversations from an oral history with mutual aid network organizers, technology ethnographers, and entrepreneurs in the public and private sectors.

On January 8, 2020, Chinese scientists identified the novel coronavirus behind a cluster of pneumonia cases originating in the megacity of Wuhan. Over the next two weeks, new cases spread from the province of Hubei across mainland China. On January 23, China's central government imposed a lockdown on Wuhan; the next day it would expand the lockdowns to encompass nearly sixty million residents of cities across Hubei.

Tricia Wang (tech ethnographer; cofounder, Last Mile): As a sociologist, I study how communities form—and particularly how trust operates differently online. That's been my focus in China for the last decade. We started hearing about the virus in Wuhan in January—that's where my fieldwork was based. When lockdowns began, residents began forming networks through WeChat called *xiao qu* (小区), which I translate to "hyperlocal groups." Even hundreds of people living in the same building had to meet each other online because their lives depended on it. And so they organized. They helped each other.

This was how China beat the virus. No one talks about it because it's bottom-up, but I know from my research it was critical to everyone's lockdown experience. From day to day, you relied on your *xiao qu* to understand "Where do I get food? Where do I find a hospital if I'm sick? How do I buy vegetables?" Everything had to be organized within the *xiao qu*. Previously, they were neighbors who didn't really know each other. Soon they were spinning off separate groups for childcare and exercise groups. That's when I realized that this is coming to America.

On March 11, 2020, the World Health Organization declared Covid a pandemic. By nightfall in the United States, sporting events had been canceled, and bans on public gatherings had been announced. In New York City—the epicenter of America's first wave—neighborhood groups such as Astoria Mutual Aid and Bed-Stuy Strong began to form. One of their tasks was sourcing personal protective equipment (PPE) for frontline health workers.

Tricia: I started to experiment, creating a hyperlocal group in Brooklyn, and then wrote a guide to starting your own group and began giving workshops because the concept was a bit weird in the United States, where you don't usually have group chats. And that's how Last Mile emerged. It was my way of adding doctors, nurses, epidemiologists, and anyone who wanted to help to our group. I quickly discovered that while many groups had already started sourcing PPE, they had no idea how to distribute it.

So we worked with disaster operations specialists and health care practitioners to design a bottom-up intelligence-gathering system to collect data on people's needs, combined with a human verification system that would call each person, get their story, and understand their nuances. At the outset, we had requests for more than three hundred thousand items of PPE, but we had only forty thousand pieces of it. We had to decide how to allocate that, so we came up with our own emergency classification system. And so on. And this was all volunteer based! And I hadn't even met nor did I know half these people!

People around the country wanted to help, so we established eight Last Mile groups in Los Angeles, Boston, Chicago, New Orleans, and Native American nations. For our next phase—which we're figuring out right now—we're moving to a community-based model, trying to work with local organizations to distribute and collect public health information along with masks. We're trying to make up for the lack of data at the hyperlocal level because all pandemics start locally—they don't start as national disasters.

While New York City networks such as Last Mile mobilized members' considerable contacts and resources, smaller groups elsewhere turned to simpler tools to jump-start their own efforts.

Stephany Hoffelt (cofounder, Iowa City Mutual Aid): The previous fall we'd talked about what a solidarity network would look like for Iowa City. We had some folks with DSA [Democratic Socialists of America] and a couple of other groups in town. I had previous street medic training, and we'd already trained a group of people who were going to act as wellness volunteers. Things like that. Then Covid happened, and we said, "Hey, remember that thing we talked about doing? Now would be a good time."

That's when we decided, "All right, we'll set up a Facebook page." There were only six of us, you know? So we put together this Facebook group to see if we could get more people interested in helping. And it just kind of spiraled from there.

Organizing was difficult at the onset because we couldn't be together and people had varying levels of skill in navigating the internet. We were just kind of winging it. The Facebook group turned out to be a nightmare—you had to link people to this and link people to that.

Now, we use a workspace collaboration tool where everything can be in one spot. We kept the Facebook page because every once in a while, we needed to put out a survey or a form for people who need help. So we share a link to a Google doc on social media. It's not perfect. I don't love using Google either.

You know what's helped the most? I have an internet bundle with a phone number attached that I'd never used. We just started sharing it. Someone dug around in their attic for an answering machine, and at first, we got a lot of calls from people who just wanted to talk to somebody. But for the first few months, we only got requests at that number—no one filled out the forms. I suspect it's because some of them were undocumented and felt more comfortable calling rather than putting their name and address in a Google doc. (And the older adults just don't know how to use it.) I'm glad I have that number now.

As local groups struggled to build their own tools or repurpose free ones, established civic tech organizations such as Code for America pivoted to support them. It wasn't long before the networks and their tools began to evolve in tandem.

Meredith Horowski (senior director, Code for America Brigade Network): Our ninety-two volunteer chapters across the country comprise designers, developers, organizers, and activists. They're always looking to identify problems in their communities they can help solve with the skills they bring to the table. Ordinarily, we've got folks working on things like making shelter information available during hurricanes or partnering with local nonprofits to build their tech stack. A lot of the work already happening within the Brigade Network was a form of mutual aid: How do I take tech and my adjacent skills and bring those to bear on the needs of my community? During the pandemic, we've seen brigades set up the Airtables these networks use to take requests for grocery deliveries, medicines, and such.

We've also seen a flip from traditional online to off-line organizing. It might start with ten thousand people clicking a petition, and then how do you move them up a ladder of engagement to do something in person and in physical space? Since 2016, we've seen a resurgence in local organizing, with people willing to risk arrest when they may have never signed a petition before. This is now happening in both directions: folks are printing out flyers with hotline numbers to pass out at farmers markets, which then kicks off the digital intake process, and others are recruiting volunteers through Facebook ads and listservs. But I think pulling people from off-line to online is more important in the architecture of mutual aid spaces and community networks because a lot of these networks are organized hyperlocally.

In [Washington,] DC, it's organized by ward. We have six or seven different wards in DC, and there is a different mutual aid network for each. And then even within that, you have these pod and tenant structures arising. So you're organizing by street, you're organizing sometimes by building with folks saying "Here's what

I can offer; here's what I need." And then the network becomes a platform for coordinating that matchmaking.

The question then becomes, How do you scale? It's a flip of the top-down organizing structures where folks say, "Here's what you need to do and here are the resources to do it." I think we're seeing the reverse of that, where the challenge for us becomes, How do we understand what's happening on the ground and then filter that up and share it across networks and spaces?

Lockdowns, quarantines, and fear of contagion quickly exposed the gaps and failures of both private services and public safety nets. Many groups began operating in legal gray areas, relying on tacit knowledge to supply help while evading scrutiny.

Stephany: When things shut down, those were surviving on meals from the food bank that could be reconstituted with hot water, and a lot of convenience stores would let them in to use the microwave for that. But when the Covid pandemic hit, the city shut off all the water faucets and outdoor water supplies in town. And a lot of stores became uncomfortable with the idea of old folks coming in. While I was getting groceries one day, I ran into a guy I knew. He was standing on the corner, telling me things have been really, really hard because there weren't many people out and he wasn't collecting as much.

So, I came home and said, "Hey, y'all. This is what I want to do. And you don't have to do it with me, but it would be cool if you would." Five of us were down for that. I started making lunches—there were some programs doing breakfasts and dinners, but nobody was making lunches—and they delivered them. We're doing between twenty to twenty-five per day.

On Mutual Aid Societies and Digital-First Organizing

Early on, the city called. They were curious about our methods. I had already talked to folks who gave me the language I needed to make it sound like we were a small group of church ladies delivering food—so that laws about commercial kitchens didn't apply to us. It's one of the reasons we won't set up a consistent spot to hand out food—because that would push us out of the gray area into something else.

As the summer of 2020 progressed, groups that formed to cope with the pandemic began pivoting to address new crises—including the uprisings against police impunity in the wake of George Floyd's killing and, in Iowa's case, a powerful derecho storm system that swept through the state on August 10, damaging or destroying more than eight thousand homes around Cedar Rapids.

Stephany: I was fairly outspoken about how upset I was at the governmental and institutional response. It took a good ten days to reach the point where the Red Cross and United Way and bigger organizations were providing the support needed. There were people who sat in houses that had been blown apart for a week. And it was because they were hung up on their own red tape. They're saying "Well, we can't find an undamaged building to put them in." They're sleeping in a building with no roof! Anything you put them in would be better at this point! But they had their guidelines and their rules, and it really hobbled them.

By that time, the smaller mutual aid groups had already moved in and were feeding everybody and distributing food and clothing. Mayor Pete Buttigieg even tweeted our Amazon link, and we ended up with a lot of donated items we took down there. So we were able to respond much faster because we didn't have any of those restrictions.

Early in the pandemic, a team of former U.S. deputy chief technology officers formed U.S. Digital Response, a volunteer effort to recruit technology professionals to build mutual aid–like tools on behalf of local governments. Their first service, Neighborhood Express, enabled cities such as Concord, CA, and Paterson, NJ, to run their own food distribution. The idea was to make official relief efforts as fast and responsive as mutual aid.

Raylene Yung (CEO and cofounder, U.S. Digital Response): In the beginning, there was an open question: Can we mobilize to find fast, effective ways to help governments on the front lines with volunteers? And within days, we felt the answer was yes. Our team's been a mix of government and tech people, so we've been able to bridge that gap between our partners and the companies making the tools. Everything we do comes directly from hearing about a need from a government partner.

Our first was Neighbor Express, which is really a matching platform. On one side, you have government teams stating their needs: we need people in this area to deliver groceries to home-bound senior citizens or care packages to women and children who aren't at school. Whatever it is, they're defining the type of help that's needed. And on the other side, it's the people signing up to offer their help and skills. We built it using off-the-shelf tools, and everything in it is open source and in our GitHub repository. From the beginning, our plan was to just publish this blueprint so anyone can adopt it if they like, and we've had people in other countries ask us to adapt it for their own networks.

That's informed several other projects, including Storefront—in which the suppliers are food producers such as community supported agriculture (CSA) participants and the people signing up are families in need of food. And a similar effort involves recruiting poll workers. Once again, you have this two-sided market with volunteers offering their time, on one side, and election offices assigning them, on the other. So I think it's true of a lot of mutual aid networks that they all more or less resemble these marketplaces, with needs, on the one hand, and the help, on the other. We've definitely leaned into that and fielded requests along the way, with the team jumping on the phone to share their insights and pointing to our open-source code for anyone who needs it.

Describing mutual aid networks as marketplaces may be technically correct but rubs many activists the wrong way. It also underscores the inherent tension between the idea of mutual aid as a practice outside private services and public welfare and the biases of well-meaning volunteers.

Tricia: I don't have a lot of faith in tech to do this work; I have a lot of faith in people who work in community organizing with a tech background to build better tools. Historically, civic tech hasn't built much useful stuff. It's mainly a white community disconnected from the reality of black and brown people on the ground who don't always understand how real organizing happens. And a lot of their tools are too idealistic, reinforce racism, and are just not usable in the field. We need tools from organizers who understand this stuff—or at least have the tech savviness to articulate what their needs are. And these tools will increasingly try to capture the qualitative experiences of people as opposed to quantitative data only—the kind that are really about lived experiences and stories.

What may ultimately separate a new generation of mutual aid networks from past programs such as the Black Panthers or disaster relief efforts such as Occupy Sandy is the accelerating pace of austerity, crises, and decay. Networks are already finding new missions for after the vaccine.

Meredith: We have a saying within the Brigade Network that's germane to mutual aid networks: redundancy is critical to inclusion. That's particularly important as it relates to digital organizing and communication tools. Whether it's Slack, Signal, Airtable, or Facebook, you need to draw multiple threads together to reach people where they're at. And you'll never be entirely able to separate the in-person aspect and spaces of mutual aid. You can process requests and volunteer digitally, but you've still got to organize the actual goods and services you're distributing to your network, which is largely still happening in church basements and different community spaces. What will that look like in the future?

We're also seeing these networks—and it's true of the brigades as well—become a mechanism for more politicized action as well. Here in DC, mutual aid groups have become a platform for organizing to support tenants' rights and protest against eviction. So I think we're going to see mutual aid become an ecosystem and platform for other kinds of activism because it's so rooted in communities and people's day-to-day needs.

Stephany: This summer things were just calming down to the point where I could breathe, and then we had the George Floyd protests—and got teargassed—and then we rolled from that into the storm. Then more protests after the city council approved buying tasers for the police department—kind of the opposite of their promise to defund police—and it's just been bam, bam, bam, bam. I'm hesitant at this point because it's been raining for five days now, and I'm thinking "Wouldn't a flood be just awesome?" That would be the way it is.

On Digital Platforms in Informal Economies

Mercedes Bidart

Quipu is digital community marketplace that enables trade without money while building creditworthiness. Cofounded by Mercedes Bidart, Quipu empowers members of low-income communities in Colombia.

What Is Quipu?

Rafi: Let's talk about Quipu—a digital marketplace you founded that maps and connects local "prosumers" to create a technology-enabled trading system that promotes shared wealth creation and retention in place. Can you give an example of how Quipu works on an individual level—perhaps a personal story or anecdote—so we can visualize what it means concretely in the life of one of its users?

> **Mercedes:** Absolutely. I can tell you about Maria. She lives in Villas de San Pablo, the neighborhood where we designed Quipu's platform. Villas de San Pablo is a neighborhood of ten thousand people in Barranquilla, Colombia. Approximately 75 percent of the people who live here were relocalized to escape the armed conflict in Colombia. Some people have also been relocated because they were previously living in high environmental risk areas, and others have moved here

from slums or informal settlements located in the middle of the city.

Villas de San Pablo has more than five hundred businesses that people run from their homes. These businesses are run by families or among community members. They provide anything you might want. You'll find people that sell shoes, people that sell cakes, people that have a restaurant, people that fix computers, tailors, and whatever else you need.

This is where Maria lives. She has a family of three kids, but her income is redirected largely toward the business that she runs from her home. She sells cakes, and the majority of her clients are people that live in the same neighborhood—the neighborhood where she also buys things for her family.

In a neighborhood like Maria's, there is an existing chain of transactions in place that sometimes is interrupted by a lack of cash. Regardless, people want to buy, and people want to sell the things they have. Quipu allows someone like Maria to create a profile that makes her *visible to her neighborhood*. It's not the same if she creates a profile on Amazon, right? Maria doesn't have a bank account. She doesn't want to sell to people that are in the United States. She wants to sell to the people that are surrounding her. By building her profile on Quipu, she can reach the clients she needs. She can put up her offers and share an exact description of what she's doing. We can also expect people to already know about her. Her neighbors can buy from her using pesos, the fiat currency. Or when they don't have pesos, they can use Quipu's tokens. These tokens, or Quipu points, are used to buy items in the marketplace. With these tokens for example, she can buy meat from a neighbor who runs a grocery store. And with those tokens, he can get his roof fixed from another neighbor. That's the chain of transactions that we are enabling.

At the same time, by recording her everyday sales and purchases, Maria creates a digital history of her activity. With this data, Quipu creates an alternative credit score with which she can access financial services, even if she is unbanked or blacklisted in the credit bureau.

Rafi: How does Quipu contribute to a sense of community by facilitating this chain of transactions?

Mercedes: Frankly, I think the community is already there. People identify with the place they live. They describe themselves as being from Villas de San Pablo. They say, "I'm from this community. We know each other. We know one another." What Quipu is doing is supporting existing communities, adding a digital layer to a network that is already in place. We transform *preexisting social capital* into economic capital. I see this as a way to amplify a lived sense of community.

This is why we start by talking to the people who live where we work. From our perspective, if systems don't visualize *themselves*, they cannot transform the places they operate within—so we start by doing visualization together. If we visualize the in-place economy, if we visualize a *network*, then we can start transforming it collaboratively. And even within this visualization process, we are building community. From the first moment we start designing the platform, there is also a community being situated: people coming together to design technology for themselves.

Realizing this was huge. We started the design process by questioning our idea of what the local economy looked like and wanting to imagine a solidarity economy. *We thought there was a difference between the economy that existed and the solidarity economy we would build.* But after working with the people in the neighborhood, they showed us that the solidarity economy was already part of the local chain of transactions and that this chain of transactions was also enmeshed in practices of care. Neighbors worry about each other's well-being and don't exclusively care about their own businesses. So by understanding this, we were able to imagine how our technology could serve an existing solidarity economy and how the whole process of designing the technology might also be a way of creating community.

Origin

Rafi: What led you to start working on Quipu marketplaces? What kind of questions or circumstances were you responding to?

Mercedes: I was born and raised in Argentina—in the outskirts of Buenos Aires—and remained there in my late teens and early twenties to pursue a degree in political science at the University of Buenos Aires. During that time, I started working with an organization called TECHO, which took me each week to an informal settlement called Amancay. There was a lot of informal commerce in Amancay, and I was working specifically with women microentrepreneurs of the informal sector—advising them on their businesses and offering management, advertising, and marketing resources.

While I was working with these women, I noticed that all of them were using smartphones and technology. I also realized that they were buying and selling to one another and that they had a robust local economy with just about anything I could find in the formal economy. That's where I started to really understand what a solidarity economy looks like as a lived experience, not solely as a concept or utopia. I saw how these women supported one another—with resources, with purchases, with knowledge, etc. And so I started imagining how we could start transforming the socioeconomic system by using technology that furthered and encouraged the kind of solidarity I was witnessing in Amancay. It was a turning point for me in which I started truly recognizing the value of working from the margins and innovating together from there.

Rafi: Can you say more about what led you to work in Colombia?

Mercedes: We first started working in Colombia as a result of a connection between the MIT Leventhal Center for Advanced Urbanism (LCAU) and the Colombian nongovernmental organization Fundación Mario Santo Domingo (FMSD). Although my experience in Amancay directly inspired me, I took up the opportunity to work at FMSD's offices in Barranquilla while I was a student at MIT, and my ideas for Quipu consolidated with help from business owners of Villas de San Pablo, an 8,200-person semipublic housing project in the southwestern extreme of Barranquilla.

Codesign Process

Marisa: Can you speak about Quipu's design process in more detail?

> **Mercedes:** We started the process of design with a question: Under what conditions do place-based technologies serve community-led socioeconomic development? From there, we started a participatory action research process: a research strategy whereby the same people who benefit from the research are trained to be the researchers themselves. Once our community members were equipped, we began mapping consumption and production in Villas de San Pablo and analyzing the results together. This exercise lets us identify how the local economy interacts with the built environment. At that point, everyone really starts to see all the assets that their neighborhood has: all the things that *they* could offer *each other*. With this information, we came back to MIT and built a prototype. When we were ready to return to Colombia, we conducted a lot of workshops to see the community's response to the prototype. From there, that product iterated tons of times. We launched the beta version in July 2020 in the midst of the pandemic.

Marisa: You've spoken so far about the importance of local community partners. What about partnerships with the civil sector and the state?

> **Mercedes:** Once we developed the app and launched, partnerships are what help us scale to new communities. Working with the informal economy requires having a physical presence in the communities. What we do with Quipu to scale to new communities is to work with organizations on the

ground, like foundations or local governments, that know their communities deeply. As of September 2021, we currently have partnerships with five social organizations, two local governments, and one private company.

Marisa: What challenges did you encounter in codesigning with the community in Villas de San Pablo?

Mercedes: It's a huge challenge to work within and design for these economies. So far our first step has been to find out what assets these communities already have, and we build from there. That is how we arrived at digital community marketplaces. These are marketplaces that reflect the identity of the people that trade within them.

The biggest challenge is to incorporate our learnings quickly. In our many iterations when we're trying out the platform with the community, we need to be very fast and lean when adding new features or changes to the product. When designing with communities, you create expectations of the results you will bring, and we need to respect their time and commitment.

Marisa: Does your wonderfully granular attention to local conditions affect Quipu's adaptability to other communities?

Mercedes: As of recently, I've come to the realization that the solutions we build for Latin America might be relevant all over the world. When I was in India in 2019 looking at social housing in resettlements, the structures I saw looked a lot like social housing in Latin America—*that* is how wide the impact of these kinds of projects could be. Of course, as a designer, I know better than to aspire to a one-size-fits-all approach. What I'm talking about are models that can be adapted. Technology needs to be tweaked and tailored to meet the needs of different communities and different places.

Marisa: Do you think your participatory process had long-term implications?

> **Mercedes:** Yes! Now, the people we worked with think differently. Now, they know they can really build something from the start and that it can be functional. Our way of approaching the solidarity economy was not solely theoretical but instead rather practical. We built something that serves the solidarity economy and its futurity.

Informal Economy

Rafi: Could you describe the informal economies that you are serving and the kind of spaces they are operating within? My understanding is that Villas de San Pablo is the result of top-down design—it's an informal economy operating within a formal settlement. How then does Quipu counter or complement this top-down design?

> **Mercedes:** Quipu's model is meant to work within place-based informal economies—this includes the economies of informal settlements but also formally designed public and social housing complexes. Our focus is the informal economy in its many manifestations. Despite being 61 percent of the world economy,[1] the informal economy is not taken seriously as a space for innovation. We can safely assume that this is because it functions largely within places where poverty is concentrated. That said, poverty does not

preclude these communities from commerce. In fact, commerce in these communities involves an enormous amount of things every day. It's estimated that within informal economies, people carry out transactions worth $10 trillion annually.[2]

To clarify, when I speak about the informal economy, I am talking about a huge economy that is informal—but not illegal. These informal economies are popular economies that are connected to a place, to the identity of a community, to the environment, and to families. Often these are economies where the family might be the unit of commerce, so to speak.

Rafi: Can you talk about the relationship between public housing and informal settlements?

Mercedes: Public housing and informal settlements are mirrors of each other. They share the same social networks. Often the residents of informal settlements end up moving into public or social housing. Both are places affected by a lack of information, a lack of money liquidity/cash flow, a lack of access to capital, and a lack of visibility of their goods/services. All of these "lacks" combine into a very challenging and unviable economic structure where businesses go unnoticed/unfrequented, people don't have the cash to make the transactions they need, and the lack of information makes people vulnerable to exploitation.

Ultimately, the communities we serve are not just marginalized in the geographies of cities but economically and socially marginalized as well. People within these spaces are regularly exploited by predatory financial services. These financial services charge informal lending charges, 200 percent interest rates, microlending charges with more than 50 percent interest rates, etc. And because there is very little information available to these communities, especially with regard to financial literacy, it's immensely challenging to find a way out of this cycle.

I think of Quipu first as an alternative that helps people trade despite a cash deficit—building up their local economies—but I also think the process of cocreating Quipu opens up a necessary conversation about community members' experiences with these kinds of exploitative "services."

Marisa: One of the things I love about Quipu is that it points out the vast scale of the informal economy. Now, the venture capitalist and start-up world goes bonkers over the scalability of an app. But what does scalability look like for Quipu and for the informal economy?

Mercedes: In the urban world, one of every four people lives within informal settlements, favelas, or slums. This figure makes up 25 percent of the world's urban population and does not even include people who live in public housing or social housing neighborhoods. It's a huge number, but there are few people that take the time to design for and with these communities. It's not as profitable, so it takes a lot more effort to make a sustainable economic plan for your solutions. Obviously, this kind of financial planning requires a unique form of creativity and innovation that is not as "valued" in our societies as the kind of innovation borne from excess capital and wealth. It's not as simple as the "solutions" that are created in Silicon Valley. Instead, this kind of work requires designing *with* and *for* the communities you are serving.

But looking at the problem from an investor perspective, it's actually an extremely interesting market. It's an untapped and huge market. We made a platform that was designed with the communities we serve and that is useful for many communities that face the same challenges. It's a matter of finding the right investors that share your vision of the world and that are not only interested in economic return but also in impact return. We have traditional investors that believe Quipu is not only a good business idea but also one that can revolutionize how communities grow their economies.

Architecture

Rafi: As I understand it, Villas de San Pablo was created for primarily residential functions; in its planning, it did not anticipate that local enterprises from within the community might actually flourish. Can you talk about what this is like?

Mercedes: In neighborhoods like Villas de San Pablo, business owners with street-level access flourish the most. Those who live in upper levels of the tower are invisibilized. And for those seeking services offered by people living in the topmost levels, the situation is also challenging. As a searchable directory, Quipu levels the playing field by giving these businesses an equal amount of visibility as any other.

In our work, we face the challenge of building technology for places that are not taken into consideration in policy design and solutions design. The housing our Quipu users are living within was not designed with commercial spaces for people that work from home—or with commercial spaces at all. There is a lack of thoughtful physical design.

For many residents of these neighborhoods, housing lotteries or resettlements perhaps placed them in the fifth floor of a tower where your commerce is forbidden. You can no longer legally conduct the home-based business you previously conducted. People face these challenges. Perhaps their life is improved by having housing, but actually quality of life decreases because people's source of income is cut.

Rafi: You're pointing out how when one operates a business from a suboptimal location, visibility becomes a spatial issue—an architectural and urban challenge.

Mercedes: Yes. When you walk in these neighborhoods, you see houses that have been transformed completely into economic units. A house located on the first floor ends up being a restaurant. From there, you can imagine how much space people have to run their business and how much space they also have to live, sleep, eat, and situate their private life. The economic unit and the household are one and the same. This happens in every informal community, in every informal settlement, but it is never taken into consideration when these spaces are built. So when you walk around, it is clear people are transforming their houses. They are trying to be visible somehow. They are trying to show what they have to offer, but their spaces are not prepared for this. There's an opportunity there.

Generally, in the investments that are being done in slum upgrading—or resettling people into public housing—there is a lot of attention placed on the infrastructure with regard to access to water, sanitation, proper housing, or even the ownership of the land. However, there is not a lot of attention given to the economy of how people are actually making their living in their neighborhoods. People's labor is not taken into consideration in social programming and in the physical design of space. The space is instead being exclusively designed for you to own a house and for you to have access to basic needs and basic services.

In a way, through Quipu, we are trying to solve problems of design and the built environment by adding a digital layer to these neighborhoods. This technology repairs neighborhoods by democratizing public-private space. When you are selling on a fifth floor, you are more at a disadvantage than when you are on the first floor. But on the Quipu platform, everybody has the same position. We are trying to democratize their space and where people are located in the space.

Marisa: So Quipu, then, is restoring agency to users—a tool for self-determination.

Mercedes: As we design Quipu, it's necessary for us to recognize that technology is not a panacea. Technology won't solve everything. It's a tool, but it's not an end-all solution. We know that there are innumerable ways to improve a community's development and built environment with or without our technology. We don't think we are solving all the problems in the communities where we work. We are a complement. What we hope is that with the data we are generating, we can inform social policy and urban design and also inform how the community wants to bargain prices, how it wants to organize itself, and what it views as necessary to really transform its quality of life.

Notes

1. International Labor Organization, *Women and Men in the Informal Economy: A Statistical Picture*, 3rd ed. (Geneva: International Labour Organization, 2018).
2. J. Jütting and J. Laiglesia, "Employment, Poverty Reduction and Development: What's New?," in *Is Informal Normal? Towards More and Better Jobs in Developing Countries* (Paris: Organisation for Economic Co-operation and Development, 2009), 129–152.

On Mutualism and Care

Ai-jen Poo

Care Crisis

Marisa: What does care in the United States look like? Can you talk about America's care crisis and the communities it impacts?

Ai-jen: America is deep in a care crisis that reaches every community across the country.

We all need care. We rely on care as an infant, most of us will rely on care to age comfortably in our homes, and people with disabilities often rely on care to live independently. Care is the essential infrastructure that supports our society and economy, through all stages of life, so we can all live full and productive lives.

And yet receiving care you need is financially out of reach for most Americans. The very wealthy may be able to afford long-term care insurance—and people who have no assets whatsoever may qualify for Medicaid. However, for those in between, like millennials, there is absolutely no plan or support in place. Parents struggle to find child care they can afford, and the "sandwich generation"—people squeezed between the caregiving needs of both their children and their parents—are shouldering the cost of a broken care ecology.

This burden is falling upon the younger generations who have had to navigate a harder economic context than ever before. So many millennials—the largest population of the United States—graduated at the height of the 2008 recession and are now making ends meet in a gig economy, which offers no long-term financial security. These same millennials are navigating the early aging of their boomer parents at a moment when affordable, quality elder care is out of the question—especially if these millennials have families of their own. As a consequence, in order to finance care, people are losing their homes or are often not able to put food on the table.

By the year 2050, some twenty-seven million of us are going to need long-term care just to meet our basic daily needs, and that is a situation that will impact the entire economy and shake up every family unless we do something drastically different.

This needs to be a national priority. Unless we face this challenge and come up with the solutions we need, the care crisis will deeply interrupt the everyday hopes of everyone: young, old, or middle-aged; healthy, ill, or disabled. We all have a stake in creating a system or plan that addresses our caregiving needs; this responsibility should not rest solely on any single individual. Like it or not, we are all part of a care force that needs support. Public policy, real leadership, economic subsidies, new infrastructure—all will be part of the equation.

Marisa: In your work with the National Domestic Workers Alliance, you interact with caregivers from all over the country. How would you describe today's caregivers? What are some of the specific challenges they face?

Ai-jen: Caregivers are some of the most important people in our society. We say that they "do the work that makes all other work possible." During the pandemic, we all saw how essential this is: in some cases, caregivers were the only contact with the outside world for people who were isolating at home. Whether family caregivers caring for their own loved ones or professional care workers, their work is incredibly skilled and can be very physically taxing, and yet they show up each day to make sure that people are receiving the care, medication, conversation, and attention they need to live independent, full lives at home.

There are nearly 2.5 million domestic workers in the United States, providing the care that we need in our homes. They are nannies, house cleaners, and home-care workers, mostly women and mostly women of color: 91.5 percent are women, and 52.4 percent are Black, Latinx, or Asian American/Pacific Islander women. They are also disproportionately immigrants: 35 percent of domestic workers were born outside the United States—and many are undocumented.

Despite the critical role this workforce plays in our society and economy, these are poverty wage jobs. The average median income of a domestic worker is $15,980 a year, which is below a sustainable wage for families. On a fundamental level, until we support the basic needs of caregivers, we will have high turnover, and an unsustainable situation for our caregivers and for the families who rely upon them.

Marisa: Can you talk about how the movement for domestic workers builds both counterpower and solutions for today's care crisis?

Ai-jen: Domestic workers have been organizing for decades in local communities around the country. This means coming together, sharing experiences, learning from one another, identifying common challenges and solutions, and working together to realize change that improves the conditions of their lives. The National Domestic Workers Alliance has sixty-four local affiliate organizations and seven chapters and members in all fifty states who come together online and offline to build power, win policy change, and share resources that help navigate the challenges of work and life. We have championed and won legislation at the local and state levels and launched campaigns like Caring Across Generations to bring together all the stakeholders in the care economy. We've also developed solutions—from the portable benefits platform Alia to universal family care, a new vision for the social safety net that offers universal access to child care, paid leave, and long-term care for working families.

Marisa: Also, what I think is so powerful is how victories for domestic workers also pave a path for other workers who were also excluded from receiving basic rights during the 1930s and 1940s—street vendors, migrant workers, car washers, etc. Can you talk about the excluded worker movement and how the economic solidarity one group builds comes to be shared with adjacent groups?

Ai-jen: The pandemic has offered a great example of this. In the early days of the shutdown, people began applauding for health care workers, and then the term *essential worker* emerged. Initially, the word was meant to refer to workers in the health care system, but soon it expanded to refer to all the workers whose labor was essential to our collective ability to survive the pandemic—grocery workers, farm workers, delivery workers, and domestic workers. These are workers who were largely invisible to most, and, suddenly, there was a public awakening about their work as essential. Immediately, all the workers' organizations across union and nonunion groups began to work together to amplify the stories of frontline workers in the pandemic and push for an Essential Workers' Bill of Rights. That work continues in cities and states across the country in a campaign called Always Essential, where we are working to ensure that essential workers' needs, contributions, and well-being are front and center as we navigate the pandemic and our recovery from it.

Marisa: Has the Covid pandemic shifted the public's understanding of the critical role caregivers play—especially during times of crisis?

Ai-jen: During the Covid pandemic, caregivers have played an important role as first responders to older people and support for people with disabilities who were isolated in our new, socially distanced world. At the risk of their own families' safety, caregivers continued to work—feed, bathe, and accompany those whom they support—knowing that in many cases they were the only lifeline to some of the people most vulnerable to the virus. But it's definitely not the first time we've seen the importance of caregivers in times of crisis.

Marisa: During Hurricane Sandy, an immigrant caregiver from Barbados told me how the rains and floods threathed the safety of the older couple she continues to care for. Braving the storms, she went to their home in Staten Island, New York, and brought them to her own home so that she could continue to look after their well-being.

Ai-jen: Exactly. Jennifer's story is not an isolated incident. If things continue as they are, we will continue to see the importance of caregivers framed by moments of disaster—in particular, climate disaster. Especially with the aging of the United States—as our population of older adults increases exponentially—our attention will shift. What we've seen in the past—and might continue to see—is how caregivers are treated as heroines in moments of crisis but are not granted dignified working conditions. Care workers put their bodies on the line for us in so many ways as first responders in a nation that still does not value their work.

If anything has become clear during the Covid pandemic, it's that in this country there are millions upon millions of workers who work incredibly hard and simply cannot make ends meet. And many of those jobs are, it turns out, essential to our health, our safety, our well-being. When I think about the workforce that I work with every day—they came into the pandemic without a single paid sick day, without access to health care, with no paid time off. And ended up paying out of pocket for safer modes of transportation to not put their clients in danger, paying out of pocket for regular Covid tests until they became more available, having a hard time finding personal protective equipment, still not having have a paid sick day, having their own kids home from school struggling to online learning, and worrying about how they are going to pay the phone bill to keep the internet going to have access to online learning for their kids. And there are literally millions of workers in this position: people who are fully employed and simply cannot afford to keep themselves safe and are not even able to take care of their families. When we address the epidemic of low-wage work in America, we need more of the conversation—and action—to raise standards. Wages must be raised, and in general, the entire floor should be raised so that the workers in these fields have dignity and respect.

Marisa: Do you think that the United States is entering a moment in its history when "raising the floor" is possible?

> **Ai-jen:** I do believe that this moment of economic recovery is the single greatest opportunity we have to reset and to create the kind of policy change that will actually increase wages—raise the floor, secure the floor—and ensure economic mobility for more people in this country.
>
> Lately, I've been thinking a lot about President Biden's Build Back Better plan. The piece of the plan that I've studied most is the caregiving plan, and what it proposes is investing about $775 billion into the care economy—into supporting access to child care, paid leave, and long-term care, particularly in the home and the community. This includes prioritizing the creation of home-care jobs with living wages and economic security.
>
> This focus is very different from the usual infrastructure and jobs programs that have emerged during recessions. But there are real parallels between the care economy and infrastructure if you think about infrastructure as that which enables commerce and economic activity. What could be more fundamental

than offering actual access to child care or access to home- and community-based services for working-family caregivers? When we make these jobs good-quality jobs, not only are we securing the work of the future because these jobs can't be outsourced or automated, but also they will enable other people to get to work. They are job-enabling jobs. They make it possible for workers across sectors to get back to work, knowing that their families and loved ones are cared for. That is essential infrastructure. This is how we leverage public dollars to rethink and reinvest in the right places in the economy. That will help us get out of this dynamic of the predominance of low-wage work, especially carework, that we have been trapped in.

Caregiving and Systemized Inequality

Marisa: Can you talk about the historical reasons that contribute to the devaluing of care in the United States?

> **Ai-jen:** In the 1930s, southern lawmakers intentionally excluded domestic workers, predominantly black women at the time, from receiving the same rights as other workers—from the right to a minimum wage to the right to organize in unions and collectively bargain. This racist exclusion set the tone for how the workforce would be treated in law and policy and in our culture: treating domestic work as less than real work and the workforce as less than workers. To this day, we still refer to domestic work as "help" rather than the profession it is for millions of workers.

Marisa: You've played a key role in galvanizing change in today's domestic worker movement. Can you talk about the 2010 Domestic Workers' Bill of Rights and how it brings us to the present day?

> **Ai-jen:** The campaign to win a Domestic Workers' Bill of Rights in New York State was the result of over seven years of organizing among domestic workers locally. It was the first effort of its kind to establish protections for domestic workers in the state labor laws, to address the long-standing exclusions of domestic workers in existing state and federal laws, and to create protections that address the particular dynamics of a labor force that works in isolated conditions hidden behind the closed doors of private homes. Envisioned and won through the persistent organizing of a diverse movement of domestic workers, the campaign brought visibility to the workforce, built the capacity and power of the workforce, and expanded what's possible in public policy for domestic workers around the country. It captured the imagination of workers and organizers nationally and became the signature campaign of a young but growing movement for dignified work.

Care as Commons

Marisa: You've spoken before about a care grid, which is a provocative word choice—I love it. We think of energy grids to share electrical power. And we think of water being shared by a community. We understand those things to be part of a common good. Can you talk about how the care grid is a public good—a commons?

> **Ai-jen:** In the United States, we have not really thought about care as a commons and something that we all

benefit from. Let's take, for example, older people in the pandemic. If one person is unhealthy and at risk, then the rest of us are also all the more vulnerable. When we provide adequate care, our well-being and safety as a whole are ensured. Access to child care was essential for working women. When the pandemic took that away, it forced millions of women, especially women of color, to leave the workforce, and now we're at 1988 levels of women's workforce participation. This is a perfect example of how care is commons. Care is essential to the public good.

It's also important when we think about solutions. If we were able to bring electricity, running water, and the internet to every home in America, we should be able to bring good care to every home in America. We just need to invest in the infrastructure required—in this case, much of it is human infrastructure or capacity. The way we have to invest in the building of roads and broadband, we should be investing in our programs and workforce to ensure access to good care.

Culture and Commons

Marisa: What cultural practices can advance and sustain the idea of care as commons?

Ai-jen: Art and storytelling define humanity and allow us to dream bigger. And in a lot of ways, the disenfranchisement and vulnerability of domestic workers are fundamentally connected to the fact that they've been made invisible. So we need stories about the value of the work and the people who do it. Art and storytelling help to reach into our heart space, shift these deeply seeded narratives, and create new possibilities and new protagonists.

For example, in the 1990s, domestic workers were seen as a marginal, shadow workforce. Now, their precarious working conditions mirror those in much of America's gig workforce. It's time we tell a new story about the work: how it is essential, how it is skilled, and how it deserves protection and inclusion in our safety net. This will help pave the way for other workers who work in nontraditional settings to also be recognized and included.

Seniors have been seen as a special interest group and are referred to in a condescending way. Right now, 20 percent of the United States' population is over the age of sixty; that's a defining characteristic of our country and the majority of our electorate, our work, and our families! So we need to mainstream the realities and humanity of older people, their specific challenges, and what they contribute and need in order to be a part of a future we can all be proud of.

Art and storytelling help create the context for new attitudes, new ways of making meaning, and new opportunities for change. To strengthen the care grid and create more affordable care options, cultural change and design have to be a central part of *any* strategy. Art has the power to break through barriers of fear and uncertainty and put us in a space of imagination and possibility.

Essays

Architecture for New Collectives

Rafi Segal

Architecture gives form to social patterns. The design of a house reflects an idea of living translated into a physical structure: the arrangement of walls, rooms, openings, and hallways enables the routines of daily life. Similarly, the design of a neighborhood reflects a vision of community life and relationships between a group and its members, whether a household, a family, or an individual. For instance a neighborhood of single-family homes laid out along streets radially converging at a place of worship manifests the centrality of religiosity in that neighborhood. Ultimately, spatial relationships are fixed by urban and architectural forms—from streets to buildings to bricks and mortar—in a way that reflects a mutual understanding of how a community ought to live for a foreseeable future.

Unsurprisingly, both the patterns of our lives and the ways we use space often change faster than the structures we construct for these uses. For example, starting in the late twentieth century, demographic and social changes displaced the primacy of the nuclear family as America's defining social unit.[1] Yet designs for North American suburbs today are still dominated by the ideal of the (white) nuclear, single-family home. *In other words, architecture is slow to respond to social change—cities even slower.* Whether the result of technological, economic, political, social, or environmental forces, such changes often take place much faster than we can plan, construct, and conscientiously redesign our buildings and cities.

In the early twenty-first century, we are witnessing shifts in our social patterns that reflect stark inequalities of late capitalism, a weak public sector, and the growing mistrust of public institutions and governance. Alongside these macroeconomic and geopolitical shifts, the proliferation of online economies, digital technologies, and new notions of community alter the ways in which we live, work, and build relationships with the people around us. More recently, the lack of faith in the state's ability to manage and protect our health during the Covid pandemic and the ensuing economic hardship accentuated the urgency to create mutual aid networks. Within a matter of months, our work-live habits dramatically changed, transforming how we understand the separation between the workplace and the domestic sphere. Right now, we are just beginning to realize the role that architecture can play to address the implications of these changes. Will our downtowns ever again be dominated by the conventional single-use office tower? Will the design of our homes, even of small apartments, begin to include a designated work space? These are but a few of the questions we face.

Still operative today, some of the legacies of these undeniable transformations include outmoded concepts such as the traditional binary between public and private. Defined by the state and by law, notions of public and private are part of an inheritance that needs to be challenged. As Michael Hardt and Antonio Negri state, "Private property is not the foundation of freedom, justice, and development, but just the opposite: an obstacle to economic life, the basis of unjust structures of social control, and the prime factor that creates and maintains social hierarchies and inequalities."[2] In other words, the American idea of private property as "inalienable" and "sacred" is deeply rooted as a fundamental civic right that carries both freedom and liability.[3]

Yet we should not confuse the potentially damaging notion of private property with privacy itself. Privacy is a condition essential to our functioning as social beings. In 1976, Irwin Altman defined privacy as the "selective control of access to the self" and made the notable distinction that privacy is not just "behavioral" but also a "psychological experience" of positive attributes.[4] Indeed, the capacity to open and close ourselves to others—that is, to act socially—is a practice of access to the self. Through this form of personal autonomy, we nurture the parts of ourselves that require solitude in order to thrive: the release of emotions, self-evaluation, experiences of safety, and freedom from observation and judgment.[5] By caring for our "desired degrees of privacy," Altman contends, we are better prepared to engage in communication with others.[6]

Privacy, however, is not just a physiological condition but also a spatial condition. In its simplest expression, privacy requires a form of physical and spatial displacement from others, a visible or material boundary that grants us control.[7] Elaborating on Altman's thoughts, Jon Lang discusses personal space as a "biological condition" that manifests differently along cultural, temporal, and social lines when applied to human life.[8] For Lang, privacy is understood functionally and as an ingredient in human health, safety, and psychological development. He refers to personal space as the distance that animals of the same species commonly maintain among themselves except for the most intimate interactions.[9] Privacy therefore is not absolute; within a spectrum of privacy—such as intimacy—we can allow someone to enter our personal space.

An innate human need for the territorialization of space and its personalization anchors Lang's sense of what is "good" or "healthy" for humans. If personal space is an "imaginary boundary" around the body that we carry with us, personalized space is achieved through the act of claiming a physical space to ourselves. According to Lang, this behavior is a "manifestation of a desire for territorial control and an expression of aesthetic taste".[10] The aesthetic aspect of this act of claiming space interests me here: beyond merely marking territory for purposes of survival, control, orientation, or reference, the aesthetic gesture affords both the establishment of identity and the construction of a memory through a personalized arrangement of the space and the artifacts assembled within.

It should be clearly noted that my interest in privacy here stems from its critical role in any exploration into collective living and that collective living, contrary to popular belief, in no way requires the weakening or elimination of private or individual life. Instead, by resituating private life within collective life-forms, we align both privacy and conditions of individuation with the health, well-being, and sustainability of the collective—a condition that I argue is also vital for our well-being. We can even argue that in many cases, and particularly for certain groups in our society, collective living can help secure better conditions of privacy. This is not a new idea, as Dolores Hayden notes in relation to the nineteenth-century American home, "Instead of sacrificing individuality and independence, the combined household can be designed so that members shall have more privileges and privacy than can be obtained in isolation."[11] Her description of "a household [that] can be conducted in such a way" is, in other words, a call for design to change social patterns.[12]

While historical precedents of collective living interrogated notions of privacy, the emergency of today's sharing economy has shaken even socially conservative mainstream norms for what can be shared. Shared home rentals (Airbnb/Couchsurfing/Love Home Swap), for example, redefine approaches to property, ownership, access, and the social relations between public and individualized space.[13] Yet the majority of these shared living spaces and other cohousing, coliving, and collective housing initiatives are predominantly shoehorned into ill-fitting architectural spaces built to accommodate other values. These outmoded architectural forms impede wholly new ways of socializing, mutualizing, and forming equity.

Responding to hyperprivatization and an erosion of the public sphere, today's *new collectives* organize around different values, functions, and modes of engagement to mutualize housing, care, labor, or financial assets. These new collectives are voluntary and dynamic groups of people who share a belief that mutualism and equality advance and protect democratic values. Porous in structure, these collectives are designed to expand and contract in terms of both members and functions—economic, environmental, and/or social—and thus easily enable participation in multiple communities, each with its new form(s) of sharing.

Unlike the all-consuming communal approaches of their predecessors—closed communities that demanded commitment to the sharing of all functions of life—and different from exploitative gig economy platforms, new collectives are distinguished by an interrogation into the fundamental question of who makes decisions and how, who receives access, and how wealth, power, and knowledge are shared.

New collectives have the capacity to combine the scale and instantaneous connectivity of digital platforms with the kinship of physical space and face-to-face interaction. Thus, architecture can play a key role in anticipating the dynamics and enabling equity in what Marisa Morán Jahn and I are calling *topo-digital* communities[14]—that is, place-based communities formed and maintained through digital platforms.

An architecture for new collectives therefore presents a more open-ended approach to where and how communities are formed and operate. Such an architecture proposes to replace the binary condition of either public or private with an expanded field of multiple in-between collective conditions. *At its core is a simple proposition: the single line dividing "mine" and "theirs" is to be replaced by a field, a gradient of spaces and conditions designed with and for what is "ours."*[5]

An architecture for new collectives suggests principles of design to serve a group of individuals and/or households rather than a single family or a single individual. This approach in no way negates or calls for the elimination of private space, nor does it seek to replace the idea of public space. Instead, an architecture for new collectives *resituates private and public along a wider scale of conditions, thus creating (and occupying) new in-between spaces and establishing new spatial relations.* This approach can be expressed across scales from the design of a neighborhood, a building, a shared space, or a room to even the design of appliances. A kitchen, for instance, can be designed to accommodate the specific needs of non-family-related individuals who use it while affording a communal aspect as well. Even an ordinary appliance like a refrigerator can be designed differently—with separate drawers for multiple users rather than a single door. Common to all of these cases is that individual and personalized decisions take place within the framework of a community and manifest themselves in individualized concrete spatial forms and across a variety of scales.

Designing gradients of access can be scaled. For instance, a new neighborhood can have an overarching and cohesive architectural design of houses and shared spaces while leaving room for the residents to personalize aspects of their own homes. The shapes and forms of the houses and the overall layout of such a housing cluster can include shared space—courtyards, storage areas, and multipurpose communal rooms, among others. A parallel architectural design process can facilitate engagement with tenants on the interior layout of their individual units.

The participation, involvement, and responsibility of the collective and the architect in the design process prove cardinal to the cohesion between the collective and its space.

If a collective is not engaged directly in the design process, its own formation and self-perception as a place-based system are jeopardized. This engagement, however, must also be meaningfully and carefully structured.

Working together with the architect, the group can define a process that enables both to arrive at an understanding and definition of the programmatic and functional needs of the project at hand. The architect's role, however, is not just to help the group define the kind of spaces it needs but also to make sure that the complete design contains the scale and variety of shared spaces alongside private and individualized spaces for group members. A coliving residential project, for instance, will raise fundamental questions as to the nature and function of spaces: Would each room have its own bath? How many people would share a kitchen, and how should this space be designed to best facilitate a common use with minimum conflicts? What are other potential shared spaces that can be used that are particular to the group?

In addition to balancing the guarantee of privacy and personalization within a communal framework, design and architecture must acknowledge and leave space for unexpected encounters and experiences. Architects and designers need to know what and where *not* to design and to acknowledge the spaces and parts of a design that should be left to the user's personalization.

In other words, an architecture for new collectives necessarily demands dialogue between the architect, the collective, and individual occupants throughout the design process.

Conclusion: Principles of Design

To summarize, I'd like to propose a set of design principles that serve an architecture for new collectives. These principles are not equal in their impact on the overall design, nor are they necessarily unique to what we might call a collectivist architecture. They are deduced from my own design work, experience, and research.

As a primary concept, *spatial gradient* allows us to move away from a binary division of private-public space and construct the architectural project as a series of spaces designed for different degrees of sharing. This approach does not necessarily strive for a blurring of boundaries between spaces; rather, it conceives the architectural work as a sequence of defined spaces assembled to serve patterns of use and different degrees of social interaction, thus resituating what is private and what is shared. In designing such a gradient, I have been using the following spatial categories:

- Private: the individualized units or intimate spaces designated for individuals, couples, or families.
- Semi-share: spaces shared among a small subgroup of individual units.
- Group-share: spaces shared by the entire building or cluster.
- Public: spaces shared between the collective, other collectives, and the broader public sphere.

These different spatial categories are not necessarily organized around a linear progression from the most public to the most private. Moreover, a collectivist approach to the design of space can lead to multiple types of connections between different and varied spaces, allowing for a diversity of interaction and use. This requires that some rooms and spaces for example have multiple entries, providing flexibility in terms of both access and function. An example of this is Carehaus Baltimore (see "Carehaus: Designing for Care" in this book), the United States' first intergenerational care-based cohousing project. Carehaus's layout serves multiple programs through various access points to enable flexibility of access and function. Separate ingress and egress points enable Carehaus to adapt to pandemic conditions.

Not merely limited to the interior of the building, the logic of a spatial gradient can govern the shape of the building in an urban space to establish a more integrated relation between the building and the city.

The *building as an integrated object* is the second principle that follows, where the designed structure is seen not as an isolated object in the city but rather as one that is intrinsically linked to its surroundings.

In my own work, this principle draws inspiration from the winning design proposal for the National Library of Israel, conceived as large urban steps that echo the topographic landscape of the Jerusalem hill on which it is located. As a public project that rethinks the role of the library in the twenty-first century, the design combines multiple collective and private functions through an integration of open and interior spaces that create multiple "centers" for different uses and different user groups. While the building's layout (in plan) may be initially read as a single large open space, it is in fact spatially subdivided into smaller defined spaces, as seen through the building's sections. Degrees of differentiation and separation between spaces are balanced with seamless connections between them. The *integrated object* principle assures an essential dual condition: the building reads as part of its urban context while maintaining its individual expression as an object of design.

User engagement, another key principle, assumes a collective involvement in the creation and management of the project. The collective—the group for which the project is being designed—becomes an active participant in the project. This participation can take place at various stages of a project: the establishment of the building's program usage (conceptual predesign stage), the design or construction process, the management of space, and the active shaping of parts over time (personalization). Here, architecture plays a significant role in identity formation. Through user engagement, individuals and groups develop a stronger sense of community and belonging. Such an approach demands a change in the traditional relationship between designer and user.

Nonuniform repetition primarily refers to the facade, envelope, or outward appearance of the building that seeks to balance the collective and the individual: in other words, to visually and spatially express the aesthetic of collectivist architecture as a whole made of separate and different individual units. While repetitive patterns are too uniform and stochastic forms lack aesthetic cohesion, nonuniform repetition expresses a collectivist subjectivity and reflects the balance between the group and the individual.

Today the synthesis of digital space and culture suffusing every aspect of our daily lives presents unique opportunities to design spaces that enable and promote the formation of new social groups in a rapidly changing world.

Through these four principles and the design approach they reflect, we can begin to understand and address the growing concerns of today's new collectives: how new social groups in need of space can form, operate, and sustain themselves. The principles outlined here allow new collectives both the place and the ground from which to thrive. As such, architecture creates social patterns.

The Next Kibbutz project is an ideal testing ground for implementing varying degrees of shared spaces to enhance community interaction while allowing individuals and families to have control over their privacy. The new neighborhood of forty-four homes in Kibbutz Hatzor, Israel, is composed of eight home clusters organized around a shared open space with storage and common rooms at the corners. This axonometric drawing of one cluster delineates a spatial gradient ranging from common spaces (light gray) to the most private spaces (black). Rafi Segal A+U, 2020.

Co-design workshops with Kibbutz Hatzor residents on the interior arrangements of homes. These co-design sessions direct user engagement towards individual's relationships within the group cluster. Photos: Gili Merin, 2016.

These existing pedestrian paths in Kibbutz Hatzor, Israel, create a network connecting all the kibbutz neighborhoods, houses, common facilities, and open spaces. These paths form the primary urban system of circulation and meeting. Vegetation and landscape along the paths screen the homes and patios to allow varying degrees of privacy and intimacy within a continuous open space. Photos: Gili Merin, 2016

140

A new neighborhood of attached family houses, Kibbutz Hatzor, Israel, 2010–2018. Six clusters of eight homes, each organized around larger shared courtyards that connect to the kibbutz network of pedestrian paths. Cars remain on the perimeter road and do not cross through the open space, in keeping with the historic design of the kibbutz. Established in 1946, Kibbutz Hatzor is situated in southern Israel near the town of Ashdod with a current population of approximately 650. Rafi Segal A+U

An MIT team led by Rafi Segal worked with masons, local brick manufacturers, villagers, MIT and Rwanda University architecture students to build a low-cost prototype village house. Photo: Ben Segal, 2017.

MIT team included: Andrew Brose (teaching assistant); students: Monica Hutton, Mary Lynch-Lloyd, Ching Ying Ngan, Taeseop Shin, Maya Shopova, Danniely Staback, Daya Zhang. Collaborators: MIT-Africa, MIT-Tata Center, Rwanda Housing Authority, SKAT Consulting, Strawtec company.

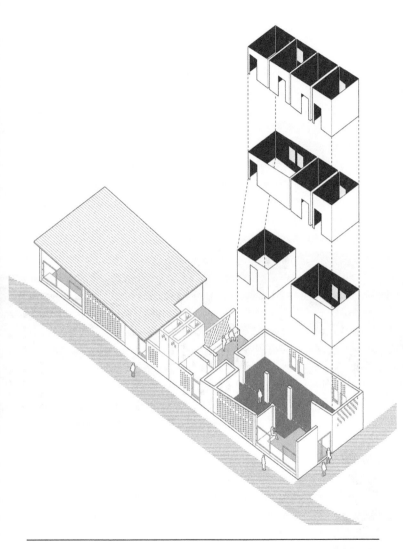

Axonometric drawing of a prototype village house designed by the MIT Rwanda workshop led by Rafi Segal. In spite of its small size, the house is designed with a variety of shared spaces depicted in shades of gray (the lighter the gray indicates more shared spaces). The private bedroom area (black) can be personalized in size and number through the self-assembly of industrialized straw panels as room partitions.

Photo by Rafi Segal, 2018.

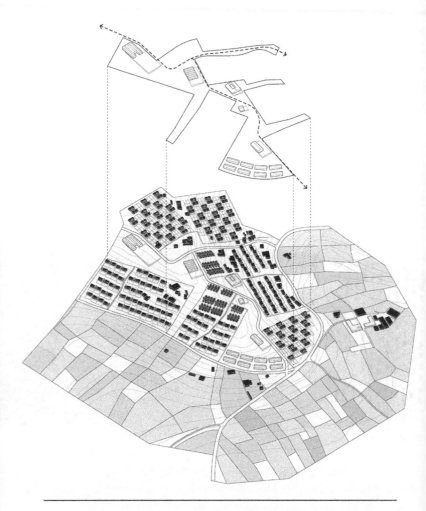

Drawing of the Mageragere village master plan prepared by the MIT team led by Rafi Segal. The project's collaborating partner, the Rwanda Housing Authority, has been modernizing and upgrading existing villages by improving infrastructure, public amenities, and services such as health clinics, job training, school rooms, village market, and collective chicken and cow sheds. A central spine (shown above) depicts the collective open spaces and shared amenities forming the new village design.

Model of Mageragere village master plan design by MIT team led by Rafi Segal

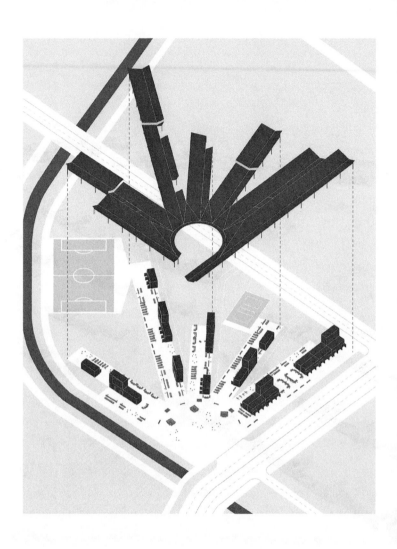

Axonometric view of the Quipu market showing the openness and flexibility of a community-based market space. Located in Villas de San Pablo, Barranquilla Colombia, a planned neighborhood designated to solve the spatial informality for refugees from civil conflict and natural disaster. The proposed physical market space supports and co-exists with the Quipu digital trading platform. The physical market space mitigates the challenges caused by unequal conditions of running businesses for homes and lack of proper support equipment. Rafi Segal A+U, 2020.

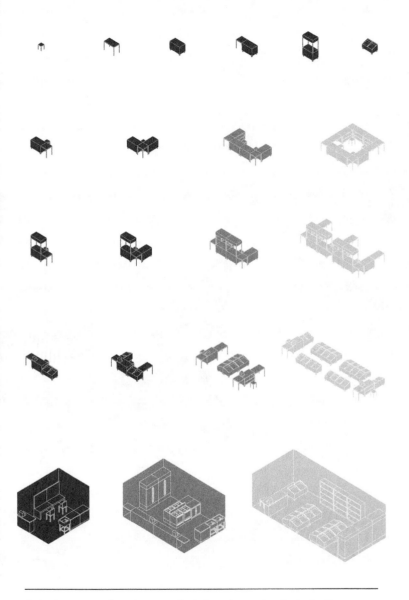

Quipu's communal market space is designed as an incubator for the local economy and community welfare. The design of modular furniture, stalls, rooms, and spaces allows combinations to support vendors across different types and needs while providing opportunities for vendors to share resources. Rafi Segal A+U, 2020.

The winning proposal for the National Library of Israel in Jerusalem conceives the building as a "landscape of stone steps" that ascend the bedrock and resonate with the surrounding terraced hills. Rafi Segal A+U, 2012.

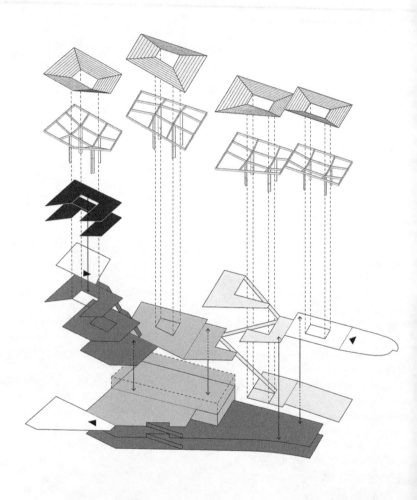

An axonometric drawing of the winning proposal for Israel's National Library reveals the sequence of collective spaces organized around open courtyards. This spatial gradient is defined by the building's structure and supported by its circulation of shared space that includes a public plaza (depicted in white) through the exhibition and cultural areas (light gray), the reading room and music center (dark gray) and the most restricted administration wing (black). Rafi Segal A+U, 2012.

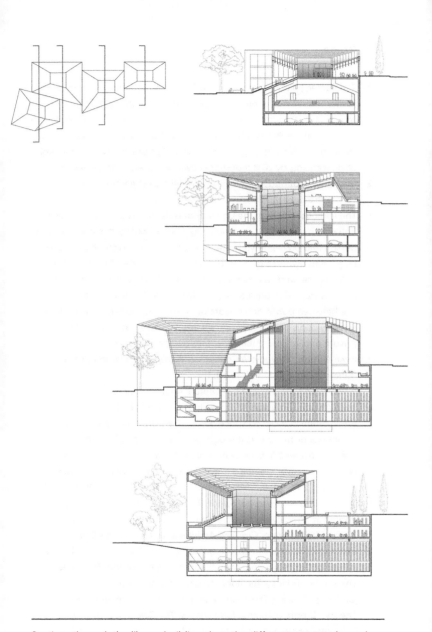

Sections through the library building show the different courtyards, each allowing light and air into the interior spaces. The courtyards and their adjacent spaces create intimate spaces within the larger open floor plan. Rafi Segal A+U, 2012.

Notes

1. Kim Parker, Juliana Menasce Horowitz, and Molly Rohal, "The American Family Today," Washington DC: *Pew Research Center*, 2015, accessed March 13, 2021.Today it is clear that in the United States there is no longer a dominant family form. Two-parent households are declining: in 1968 married couples with at least one child comprised nearly 70 percent of all households; by 2018 that share has fallen to less than 30 percent.

2. Michael Hardt and Antonio Negri, *Multitudes* (New York: Oxford University Press, 2017), 85.

3. The litigious culture in the United States demands precise boundaries between ownership to ascertain legal responsibility. If, for example, a person falls on a sidewalk due to unmaintained pavement, responsibility—and ownership—must be determined in order to demand repair or to secure funds for medical treatment. However prosaic this example may be, it demonstrates not only the precise demarcation of the line between public and private but the implications of this condition on individuals and groups. Within this worldview, knowing what is private and what is public becomes a social necessity.

4. Irwin Altman, "Privacy: 'A Conceptual Analysis,'" *Environment and Behavior*, No. 8:1 (March 1976): 11.

5. Irwin Altman, "Privacy: 'A Conceptual Analysis,'" 24–26

6. Irwin Altman, "Privacy: 'A Conceptual Analysis,'" 13–14

7. Being alone in a closed space does not ensure privacy. Perhaps it eliminates disturbances through the factor of sight, but other senses are also involved in privacy making. For instance, noise can disrupt privacy. However, one also experiences extreme privacy in a vast open space like a forest, for example, despite sound/visual "disturbance."

8. Robert Sommer, *Personal Space: The Behavioral Basis of Design* as quoted in "Privacy, Territoriality, and Personal Space—A Proxemic Theory" by Jon Lang, *Creating Architectural Theory: The Role of Behavioral Sciences in Environmental Design* (New York: Van Nostrand Reinhold, 1987), 145–156. Lang theorizes a self-named "Proxemic Theory" on "Privacy, Territoriality, and Personal Space".

9. Jon Lang, "Privacy, Territoriality, and Personal Space—A Proxemic Theory", *Creating Architectural Theory: The Role of Behavioral Sciences in Environmental Design*, 147.

10. Jon Lang, "Privacy, Territoriality, and Personal Space—A Proxemic Theory", *Creating Architectural Theory: The Role of Behavioral Sciences in Environmental Design*, 147.

11. Dorothy Hayden, *The Grand Domestic Revolution: A History of Feminist Designs for American Homes, Neighborhoods, and Cities* (Cambridge, MA: MIT Press, 1981), 36.

12. For further reading see: H. Sohn, S. Kousoulas, and G. Bruyns, "Commoning as Differentiated Publicness," *Footprint: Delft Architecture Theory Journal*, no. 16 (April 2015): 1–8.

13. Arun Sundararajan, *The Sharing Economy: The End of Employment and the Rise of Crowd-based Capitalism* (Cambridge, MA: MIT Press, 2016), 45.

14. The term "topodigital communities" was conceived with Marisa Moran Jahn.

15. The concept of "gradient spaces "was developed in a research-design seminar titled "Collectives" first taught at MIT's School of Architecture and Planning by Rafi Segal in Fall 2016.

Creation as Counterpower

Marisa Morán Jahn

We're rumbling along in our bright orange, decked-out 1976 Chevy van when a lizard scurries across the road, sending us careening to a full stop. My son Choco starts sneezing up a storm, which we attribute to the arid desert.

We pull off the 66 to gas up. The station attendant mouths the words emblazoned on our van's hood and sides: "NannyVan: Accelerating the movement for domestic workers' rights nationwide." He smiles and we wave back. We climb back into our mobile studio and Anjum Asharia, my copilot, rolls the van's vintage door shut with careful finesse to keep it from careening off its track. Buckling up, we realize the erstwhile brake-stop had upturned a flask of Cajun seasoning, sending up a plume of spice irritating to a baby's sensitive nose. Choco's stopped sneezing by now and the engine lulls him to sleep, allowing the rest of us get to work. Together with Anya Krawcheck, an actress and nanny, I smooth out some of the choreographic wrinkles of the roadside dance we will soon perform. Marc preps our camera gear. For now, Anjum takes the helm.

Heading back toward the highway, the guys in the *ranflas* (Chicano for *lowriders*) give us the thumbs up, appreciating our antique ride. Out here along the Arizona border, everyone knows someone who is or was a nanny, house cleaner, or caregiver because that form of informal labor is often the first job to which new immigrants turn. Most, however, are not familiar with the term *domestic worker*.

Designed by Marisa Morán Jahn (Studio REV-) with members of the National Domestic Workers Alliance, the NannyVan (2014–2016) is a mobile studio that accelerates the movement for domestic workers' rights. Photo by Marisa Morán Jahn.

As a pop-up, place-making project, the NannyVan unfolds in parks, transit stops, schools, and public spaces where domestic workers (nannies, housekeepers, caregivers) convene to exchange stories and resources. Photo by Marc Shavitz, 2014.

Across the United States, 2.5 million women work as nannies, housekeepers, and caregivers for the old, young, and disabled. While the definition of a domestic worker varies from state to state, in reality, these workers fluidly shift roles.[1] In the words of Marlene Champion, a New York–based caregiver who has worked for fifty-seven years, "We are like a fruit cocktail. We are caregivers, teachers, nurses, companions—you name it, we are that role."[2] Adding to this list, the Covid pandemic brought attention to domestic workers' role as frontline workers, risking their health and families' safety while continuing to care for other people's children and older parents.

CareForce One designed by Marisa Morán Jahn (Studio REV-) with Caring Across Generations and the National Domestic Workers Alliance, 2016–2018. Photo by Marisa Morán Jahn.

And yet, over and over in our travels—more than ten thousand miles in the NannyVan as well as in my second ride, the CareForce One, I saw the conspicuous absence or omission of domestic labor in culture, law, and language. This failure to formally recognize a central part of society registers in personal narratives such as this: "I've been working as a nanny for the past fifteen years but never identified as a domestic worker or someone entitled to basic rights." As family members shared, "My mother cleaned houses when I was a kid, but I just thought of it as an extra gig she did for money; I didn't realize it was so widespread." From those who employ caregivers we heard: "Until my family needed care, domestic

INCREASE PRE-TAX CARE ALLOWANCES!

Since 1986, childcare costs have risen 70% but the pre-tax allowance for dependent care has stayed the same.

workers were entirely *invisible* to me." As Miranda Fricker points out, these "absences of proper interpretations, blanks where there should be a name for an experience which is in the interests of the subject to be able to render communicatively intelligible" contribute to a broader perceptual and interpretive blindness, or "hermeneutical lacuna."[3] On a systemic and accumulative level, the lacuna reifies "hermeneutic injustices [that] actively contribute to a persistent and widespread marginalization."[4] In other words, *not* to see and *not* to recognize are not simply neutral but an active form of perpetuating injustice.

The question of how we might then "see" and value domestic labor guides my decade-long collaboration with the National Domestic Workers Alliance, Caring Across Generations, and other regional and hyperlocal groups organizing caregivers and care receivers. I'm interested in how art can undo this (hermeneutical) lacuna—this lack or deficit that fails to recognize the centrality of care. In other words, how can art enable us to both "see" and build the tools, structures, and imaginaries for a vibrant, just future? In sharp critique of the dictum that design is neutral, this aggregate body of work

---

Marisa Morán Jahn.
Increase America's Pre-Tax Care Allowance, 2017
Silkscreen print, 19" × 25"

In the United States, most workers received their basic rights in the 1930s and 1940s (New Deal Era), but several Southern lawmakers intentionally excluded domestic workers because they were largely African American. Propaganda posters created during the New Deal Era used highly stylized graphics and civic-minded language to promote nationalism, public health, and other social values. Jahn's CareForce silkscreen print series appropriates New Deal era visual language and style but instead galvanize Americans to build bottom-up movements, eliminate discriminatory policies, and chart new solutions to help solve the United States' care crisis."

that I call *CareForce* self-reflexively queries the very relationship between counterpower and creation. Creation—or art, design, architecture, media, and stories—together with counterpower—a form of power firmly anchored in historicity and futurity—has the capacity to transform our experiences and forge collective self-determination.

Movement-Building and Counterpower

Along my journeys, several of the women I met in the South come from a long and proud line of caregivers stretching back to when their great-great-great-grandmothers were slaves. Since that time, domestic workers have faced repeated legal exclusion contributing to their economic precarity. After the Civil War, when slavery in the United States was ostensibly abolished, 90 percent of African American women worked as housemaids and caregivers because they were legally barred from holding other professions reserved for Whites.[5] In the 1930s and 1940s—a period generally known for its progressive labor policies—southern lawmakers intentionally prevented domestic workers, street vendors, car washers, migrant workers, day laborers, and other predominantly Black labor groups from receiving the same rights as other workers. This willful, systematic exclusion embodies what Harney and Moten characterize as state-driven policies whose "exclusive and exclusionary uniform/ity of contingency [is presented] as imposed consensus, which both denies and at the very time seeks to destroy the ongoing plans, the fugitive initiations, the black operations, of the multitude."[6] In this playbook of racially motivated statecraft, those (seeming or presenting themselves to be putatively) in power proffer various excuses as to why the state cannot provide domestic workers decent wages or protect them against workplace injuries, sexual

Ai-jen Poo (left) and Marisa Morán Jahn (right), 2016. Photo by Marc Shavitz.

harassment, or trafficking. Insurance companies, lobbyists at different points in history representing the au pair industry, or in a different era—slave masters—explain that doing so would bankrupt the economy, make care too expensive, eliminate third-party care providers, and/or violate the principle that the government has no right to regulate the privacy of its citizens' homes.

Parallel to this dominant narrative runs a long and proud history of movement building led by domestic workers. Moments when this vector of counterpower surfaces include the strike in 1881 by three thousand washerwomen in Atlanta, Georgia, that won them a wage increase;[7] Dorothy Bolden's leadership in organizing twenty-five thousand women as "household technicians" in the 1970s;[8] the peaceful refusal of activist and domestic worker Rosa Parks, which furthered the civil rights movement; and the momentum for racial equity accelerated by the Black Lives Matter movement co-founded by a queer Black nanny from Oakland, California, named Alicia Garza.

Within this trajectory, a significant achievement transforming domestic work today was led by activist Ai-jen who organized domestic workers to share their stories with lawmakers in New York's state capital. Led by predominantly immigrant women, the seven-year long campaign resulted in the passage of the nation's first Domestic Workers' Bill of Rights in New York State in 2010.

This victory inspired other domestic workers to organize and pass labor protections in *their* states. Each campaign and each victory began through the very simple and precious act of sharing a story whose utterance at times comes with a great cost, as Proust aptly captured in his dictum, "Narrate or die."[9] The urgency of storytelling forms the crux of *1001 Nights*, whose central protagonist, Scheherazade, saves her life and those of countless others by sharing her story. As *1001 Nights* allegorizes the triumph of life over death through storytelling, the same was true in this movement for domestic workers' rights where stories *matter*. Reciprocal and infectious, storytelling builds counterpower.

Soon after the passage of the New York Domestic Workers Bill of Rights, a local advocacy organization, Domestic Workers United, reached out to me and my art and journalism team to help inform the state's two hundred thousand nannies, housekeepers, and caregivers about their newfound rights. Embracing this challenge with relish, I began poring through the legal language with lawyers and advocates including my own cousin, Carmela Huang. Alongside various policy tool kits I codesigned, I also sought to use transmedia strategies to spread the word farther.

At the time, radio was quickly obsolescing, smartphones were not financially accessible to domestic workers, and print literacy among this highly international workforce was low. Seeking alternative audio-based civic media platforms, we found inspiration in the West African taxi cab drivers in New York City who would dial a line to hear an individual parlay the news from back home in real time—yet we needed something accessible at any hour. TEXT4BABY, an early SMS-based messaging system from 2010 delivering timely news to pregnant mothers was another important precedent for us—yet we needed something more imaginative, delightful, and charming. Voz Mob, an open-source voice-over-internet-protocol (VOIP) platform created in 2010 by Sasha Costanza-Chock with Los Angeles day laborers at the Institute of Popular Education of Southern California (IDEPSCA) directly informed what we built—yet we needed carefully produced content whose brevity, humor, and high production value could commanded listeners' attention.

The app *we* produced—first with domestic workers in New York and subsequently with workers in Massachusetts and California—featured short-form audio-novelas whose motley of playful characters—a brassy mouthed ham sandwich, a pair of talking lungs with thick Bronx accents, a nosy Senorita Sabelotodo (Miss Know It All)—conveyed need-to-know information about wage theft, retaliation, health, safety, and more. The audio-novelas' psychedelic stylization made its content more memorable while humorously conveying the dehumanization and everyday horrors of domestic work. A similar aesthetic strategy characterized the work of early twentieth-century Caribbean Surrealists: in 1943, at the height of World War II, the Martinican poet Suzanne Césaire penned the line "Surrealism—tightrope of our hope,"[10] suggesting that only an altered state could aptly capture the era's tumult.

Take for example a recording session we held with domestic workers at Boston's Brazilian Worker Center in 2013. "I'm Clara, reporting live from the inside of a vacuum cleaner," voiced Anya into the mic, eyebrows knit together as she gets into character. On cue, a few member-leaders crowded around the second mic start cheering and hollering, trying to simulate a raucous party bus. Anya, acting as Clara, continued as if in controlled panic: "This place is packed with bed bugs and the scene here is absolutely wild. These six-legged critters are notorious for infesting the homes nationwide and drinking the blood of ordinary citizens." "And . . . cut!" I say, indicating that we'd finally achieved our perfect recording. But still in character, the bedbugs kept running with arms akimbo as if terrorizing the worker center. This frenzy then prompted another member to run around flailing her long arms, and we immediately get the reference: in a previous workshop, she'd imagined herself as a spider whose eight legs in continual motion mimic the endless tasks domestic workers juggle. We stoop over in deep, deep laughter, trying to keep from peeing our pants.

In moments like these, our laughter became bound up with self-reflexive wonder at our capacity to shake off pain and know our own strength. As Michael Hardt and Antonio Negri write, "In the face of [the] arrogance of power, the most adequate response, rather than lamenting our poor lot and wallowing in melancholy, is laughter . . . which is a sign of joy, a sign of power." Connecting laughter with commonwealth, they elaborate:

> Ours is also a laugh of creation and joy, anchored solidly in the present. Our free and equal access to the common, through which we together produce new and greater forms of the common, our liberation from the subordination of identities through monstrous processes of self-transformation, our autonomous control of the circuits of the production of social subjectivity, and in general our construction of common practices through which singularities compose the multitude are all limitless cycles of our increasing power and joy. While we are instituting happiness, our laughter is as pure as water.[11]

In other words, for Hardt and Negri, laughter builds counterpower. So, too, George Bataille identifies the unifying character of collective laughter: "Those who laugh [les rieurs] together become like waves of the sea—there no longer exists between them any partition as long as the laughter lasts they are no more separate than are two waves, but their unity is undefined, as precarious as that of the agitation of the waters."[12] Anca Parvulescu points out that for Bataille, the temporality of laughter is at once firmly anchored in a fragile present yet limitless in unifying its laughers in such a way that reverberates infinitely.[13] For us, and throughout the CareForce journey as a whole, laughter functions as a plurivocal reverberation uniting struggles and creation over time and space.

Thanks in part to moments like these, the trust I forged with my collaborators proved essential to launching our app with a success that we could not have anticipated. Invested in and proud of our work, our collaborators handed out palm cards about the app to thousands of their peers in the parks, at bus stops, and in their neighborhoods. Besides conveying urgent legal information, the app provided our teammates a departure point for exchanging stories with those who did not yet see themselves as domestic workers. Equally important, the high production value and aesthetic caliber of our project dignified its makers, ensuring stickiness, stewardship, and what media theorist Henry Jenkins refers to as "spreadability."[14] Over time, governmental organizations— from the White House to the U.S. Department of Labor to the New York City Mayor's Office to the United Nations—invited us to present our work, acknowledging their challenge in reaching informal labor sectors.

When domestic workers in other states started building movements to change laws, I sought a way to meet them where they're at. I also saw how domestic workers responded enthusiastically to the graphics I had designed for the app and felt we needed something visually bold to intrigue, delight, and capture the attention of a broader public. About a decade prior, I'd designed a few peripatetic sculptures such as *A La Carte*, a gallery on wheels resembling an ice cream cart that sold "art for popsicle prices" on the streets of San Francisco. After opening its top flaps, a crank wheel raised a stepped shelf displaying unique multiples, sound pieces, and soft sculptures made by local artists. Co-created with artist/designer Steve Shada, *A La Carte* was operated by ourselves and many of the participating artists. Whether at bus stops, parks, or museums, the cameo appearance of the charming cart was invariably met with curiosity, selfies, and many times, warm applause akin to a school mascot.

In addition to the visual allure of *A La Carte* and other "kits" I had designed, the process of setting up in public, revealing what's inside, and performing maintenance commands attention and invites dialogue. So too, for socially engaged artists like myself working in the public sphere, kits are characterized by their promissory quality, offering all the necessary (and magical) equipment needed to create artwork from circumstance.

With this and others precedents in mind, I enlisted Steve to help design an even larger peripatetic "kit" that could draw attention to the question of domestic work. He scavenged parts from seven junkyards to outfit the chassis of a 1976 Chevy van I'd bought on Craigslist. The illustrations I created for its vinyl graphics lent our ride an A Team meets Scooby-Doo meets superhero look. In various cities where we sojourned, a typical day's itinerary included rolling up to Toddler Story Time Hour at the public library, parking in front of public parks where nannies bring their kids after school, and setting up at other places where domestic workers convene to share and exchange the resources we continued to create: paper tool kits, augmented reality trading cards, short videos, and more. Choco, whose second word after "mama" was "NannyVan," had demonstrated our ride's phonetic appeal for all ages. Waddling up to the car, toddlers would in turn attract nannies and parents with whom we'd start conversations.

Embodying the artist Krzysztof Wodiczko's notion of interrogative design or Carl DiSalvo's notion of adversarial design or agonistic design,[15] the NannyVan embraced the capacity of art and design to not simply deliver an answer but instead to raise fundamental questions and provoke discourse.

For me, this journey was and continues to be rooted in a very personal experience: after the birth of my son, I found myself benumbed by the isolation of motherhood in New York City, staggering under the cost of child care despite all of my educational and institutional privileges, and anxiously anticipating how I was going to care for my aging parents. While I had worked as a caregiver for a disabled man in my twenties, I recognized I spoke more powerfully from my position as one of the 2.2 million domestic employers[16] in the United States experiencing a care crisis. As the movement for domestic workers rights is dynamic and ever-growing, my son and I continue to be engaged in new ways.

Designing Counterpower

After a few weeks in Arizona, we've finally made it to the Bay Area. I'm motioning to the NannyVan to park just a little to the left, where it will obscure the ugly parking lot fixtures and instead form a colorful backdrop for our celebration. Just warming up, we plan to commemorate the one-year anniversary of California's Domestic Worker Bill of Rights, a feat inspired by New York State's legislative victory a few years prior. Curled up on the lime green carpet and perched on the NannyVan's pop-out benches and craft carts, kids color in know-your-rights placemats providing trickle-up know-your-rights tips to the children's mamas who crowd around sharing stories and tamales. Anya doo-wops with a few women; Marc gets feedback on our policy toolkit from a few parents; Anjum asks me if I want to hold the baby or the camera.

Domestic workers celebrate the first anniversary of the California's Domestic Workers Bill of Rights, 2016. Photo by Rebeka Rodriguez.

John leads a *CareForce Disco* at a rally on steps of City Hall, Los Angeles, 2016. Participants include worker-leaders from Coalition for Human Rights Los Angeles (CHRLA), Pilipino Worker Center (PWC), the Institute of Popular Education of Southern California (IDEPSCA), and the National Domestic Workers Alliance (NDWA). Video still by Marc Shavitz.

Voices from the CareForce (2017) is a booty-shaking album that remixes the voices of domestic workers across the United States. Later, Jahn and caregivers co-choreographed various dances that narrate the history for domestic workers' rights. Produced and designed by Marisa Morán Jahn. Vocals by Guillermina Castellanos, Aquilina Soriano-Versoza, Anya Krawcheck, Narbada Chhetri, and others. Music and beats by Diana Nucera and Marijke Jorritsma.

In this pop-up public place that we cobbled together, the exchange of resources and knowledge appears casual and provisional—a spatial strategy of the undercommons. As opposed to top-down "policy," Harney and Moten point out that the undercommons mounts power through *planning* (or what activists refer to as movement building) whose productive genius takes place in informal contexts and makeshift terrain—on "any back porch, any basement, any hall,"[17] or here in this parking lot spilling out the back of our junkyard superhero ride.

Place-making initiatives like the NannyVan in fact describe the material and spatial conditions of precariats like domestic workers and identify moments that exercise agency and mount counterpower. Given that low remuneration, a paucity of capital, low liquidity, and limited access to credit are challenges precariats face, an *architecture* of the under-commons, then, is perhaps less brick-and-mortar structures (or Architecture with a capital A) and instead moreso a set of infrastructurally light *design strategies* enabling the claiming, occupying, and instauration of space. As another characteristic defining these spatial strategies, many precariats are immigrants who intend to return to their home countries or alternately don't know how long they will stay in the host country: for example, seasonal migrant workers who may have a renewable visa (but don't know whether it will be renewed), domestic workers whose visas are tied to an individual employer, or the many immigrants whose status shifts under political administrations. Given this, in terms of spatial practices, *impermanence and provisionality maintain primacy over fixity, durability, and longevity.* Another spatial practice—the ability to *shift between visibility and invisibility*—proves useful to groups struggling to achieve social recognition or seeking to evade political persecution.

To dwell on one particular example, pop-ups like the NannyVan are temporally delimited and adaptable; they expand and contract; they can pick up and move elsewhere. Pop-ups can operate as nodes along a vector or journey and may be part of a related spatial strategy—*occupying and re/claiming public space* through protests, rallies, or marches that can range from peaceful to antagonistic in tone. Through place making, pop-ups can confer safety, protection, and political momentum. At our various stops throughout the NannyVan's treks across the United States, our performative place-making proudly declared the right of domestic workers to simply *be* in public. Even if only temporarily through the experience of a pop-up, the ability to experience this human right to live without fear invites participants to envision this as a full-fledged reality. The next step is to imagine our built environment as one that fully embraces and centers domestic labor—a practice that our collaborative artwork helps to envision and realize.

Back in the parking lot, Guillermina, a talented singer and organizer, checks her mic, preparing to fire up the crowd. She turns on the amp and draws together the women around us. Guille begins belting a song she wrote about the movement, rousing the two hundred women in an animated call and response. Following her lead, I facilitate the dance I'd choreographed with caregivers in Detroit, New York, Miami, Los Angeles, and the Bay Area. Some gestures (washing windows, shaking sheets) name and describe care work. More broadly, the power of our dance lies in moving together in this space. Moving in synchrony, we point toward the horizon as if conjoining the future and present, creation and counterpower. Later I take my recording of Guillermina's song, give it a techno-glitch dance track. It sounds so good that we declare it our "Nanthem," or NannyVan anthem, and continue to play it on the streets, in marches, in courthouses, at worker centers, and in museums, carrying with it the traces of our journey and its evolving choreography.

Body Burdens and Boogying

A year later and now back home, we assemble fifty women in Corona Plaza in the heart of Queens, New York. We gather around the speaker, listening to the "Nanthem." I show them the pointing-to-the-horizon gesture, which they decide to transform by shifting their finger toward the ground to achieve a Saturday Night boogie. Moments like this drive my work as an artist: *I define success by those moments when others feel purchase to join in and improvise, when the work—porous and adaptable—takes on a life of its own.* Michel Serres describes the genuine feeling of play in a game of ball: the game is not the ball lying inert on the ground but the ecstasy when the ball passes from one player to another. "The 'we' is less a set of 'I's than the sets of its transmissions. . . . Participation is the passing of the 'I' by passing."[18] In other words, against the individualist notion of selfhood or the cult of the individual author—both fallacies perpetuated by Western capitalist modes of cultural production—cocreation hovers between *I* and *we*, signifying the commutability between singular and collective.

After rehearsing the song a few times, we play it again, now "performing." For these largely undocumented women, dancing in public can be political. During periods when federal immigration officials routinely raid these women's homes and communities, simply walking to work means risking deportation and family separation. Against this, they felt that our mobile studios and dances invoked their civic right to simply be in public and their human right to live without fear.

When the "Nanthem" ends, Vero Ramirez, a key worker leader, assumes the mic. "Don't forget to stretch!" she reminds. "Strengthening your neck and abdominals helps those back muscles you use while sweeping or lifting those you care for. We don't yet have ergonomic rights like other workers so we need to take care of ourselves." For a few weeks, we've been brainstorming how she can use our dance to communicate health and safety precautions to the women she organizes.

For context, in the United States, the Occupational Safety and Health Administration was established in 1971 to strengthen workplace protections—yet domestic workers were denied these same rights. As a result, this workforce comprised of 90 percent women and 60 percent immigrants[19] disproportionately suffers workplace injuries when compared to other vocations. What needs no explaining to my collaborators is that the current conditions of domestic labor essentially assume women of color will absorb the body burdens of late capitalism, to adapt Kathryn Yusoff's framework on the global dimensions of the biopolitical.[20] Aimé Césaire (writer, partner of Suzanne Césaire) invokes how Caribbean subjects were rendered equivalent to the commodities they energetically produced—a process that enabled and fueled the transatlantic slave trade. "We are walking compost hideously promising tender cane and silky cotton,"[21] he writes, recalling something my friend June Barrett, a Miami-based caregiver and worker leader, shared with me on our first trip to Miami: "Some people only think of us [caregivers] as wiping old people's butts," she said. "But we are more than that."[22] Erlinda Alvarez, a Filipina caretaker from Chicago, explains that when her peers in the United States pass away, their community comes together to raise the thousands of dollars needed to send the dead body home by plane so that it can be buried according to the funerary customs of the Philippines—a last attempt to recover bodily sovereignty in spite of late capitalism's cruelty.[23]

Horizons

It's now 2016, and our beloved NannyVan finally breaks down. Choco and I stand on the street, crying as we watch the tow truck take our beloved to her final destination.

ITVS / PBS INDEPENDENT LENS, SALTY FEATURES, AND STUDIO REV- PRESENT "THE CAREFORCE ONE TRAVELOGUES"
EXECUTIVE PRODUCERS: SALLY JO FIFER (ITVS) | SENIOR PRODUCER: KARIM AHMAD (ITVS) | SUPERVISING PRODUCER: PAMELA TORNO (ITVS)
DIRECTOR & DIRECTOR OF PHOTOGRAPHY MARC SHAVITZ | PRODUCERS YAEL MELAMEDE, MARISA MORÁN JAHN
CO-PRODUCER ANJUM ASHARIA | ARTISTIC DIRECTOR MARISA MORÁN JAHN
FEATURING ANJUM ASHARIA, MARISA MORÁN JAHN, LUCA LASDON ("CHOCO"), MEMBERS OF THE NATIONAL DOMESTIC WORKERS ALLIANCE
MUSIC BY THOMA CHER | RUPEN GEHRKE, FLORIAN SAGNER. REMIX BY D. HAAKSMAN | GINGEE | LAW | M PEACH | DIANA NUCERA (MOTHER CYBORG) | TRIS TAYLOR

A humorous and touching road tale, *CareForce One Travelogues* (2018) features John, her son Choco (aka Luca), and their buddy Anjum Asharia as they travel from their homes in NYC to Miami in a fifty-year old station wagon, the CareForce One. Meeting up with nannies, housekeepers, caregivers, and allies along the way, this series explores how care intersects with some of today's most pressing issues—immigration, the legacies of slavery, racial discrimination, and more. The 24-minute documentary is accessible for free: http://marisajahn.com Graphics by Marisa Morán Jahn.

After a good and proper period of mourning of several months, Ai-jen's team gives me the idea for a new ride—the CareForce One. I can't imagine a more honorific gift than this brilliant name! I scour Craigslist for months to find a befitting beauty—a vintage cream-colored 1967 Mercury station wagon with cherry red leather seats—a nine-seater to boot. Adding final touches before we head south, I adorn the sides of the CareForce One with vinyl stickers featuring portraits I illustrated of Guillermina, Narbada, Natalicia, Anya, Anjum, and other superheroes who guide my journey and transform the movement for domestic workers' rights.

A new journey has begun.

Notes

1. Linda Burnham and Nik Theodore, *Home Economics: The Invisible and Unregulated World of Domestic Work* (New York: National Domestic Workers Alliance, 2012), https://www.domesticworkers.org/wp-content/uploads/2021/06/HomeEconomicsReport.pdf.
2. Marlene Champion, interview by Marisa Morán Jahn, Ford Foundation, New York City, March 10, 2015.
3. Miranda Fricker, *Epistemic Injustice: Power and the Ethics of Knowing* (New York: Oxford University Press, 2007), 160.
4. Fricker, *Epistemic Injustice*, 154.

5. John Smith Jr., curator at the National Museum of African American History and Culture, interview by Marisa Morán Jahn, Washington, DC, February 28, 2017.

6. Stefano Harney and Fred Moten, *The Undercommons: Fugitive Planning and Black Study* (New York: Minor Compositions, 2013), 76.

7. See Tera W. Hunter, *To 'Joy My Freedom: Southern Black Women's Lives and Labors After the Civil War* (Cambridge, MA: Harvard University Press, 1999), 88–97.

8. Premilla Nadasen, "Power, Intimacy, Contestation: Dorothy Bolden and Domestic Worker Organizing in Atlanta in the 1960s," in *Intimate Labors: Cultures, Technologies, and the Politics of Care*, ed. Eileen Boris and Rhacel Parrenas (Stanford, CA: Stanford University Press, 2010), 204–208.

9. Malcolm Bowie, *Proust Among the Stars* (New York: Columbia University Press, 2000), quoted in A. S, Byatt, introduction to *The Arabian Nights: Tales from a Thousand and One Nights*, trans. Richard Francis Burton (New York: Modern Library, 2001), 24.

10. Suzanne Césaire, *The Great Camouflage: Writings of Dissent (1941–1945)*, ed. Daniel Maximin, trans. Keith L. Walker (Middletown, CT: Wesleyan University Press, 2012), 38.

11. Michael Hardt and Antonio Negri, *Commonwealth* (Cambridge, MA: Harvard University Press, 2007), 382–383.

12. George Bataille, quoted in Anca Parvulescu, *Laughter: Notes on a Passion* (Cambridge, MA: MIT Press, 2010), 90. See also George Bataille, "Laughter," in *The Bataille Reader*, ed. Fred Botting and Scott Wilson (Malden, MA: Blackwell, 1997).

13. Parvulescu, *Laughter*, 90.

14. Henry Jenkins, Xiaochang Li, and Ana Domb Krauskopf, with Joshua Greene, "If It Doesn't Spread, It's Dead (Part One)," *Confessions of an Aca-Fan* (blog), February 11, 2009, http://henryjenkins.org/blog/2009/02/if_it_doesnt_spread_its_dead_p.html.

15. Carl DiSalvo, *Adversarial Design* (Cambridge, MA: MIT Press, 2012).

16. Julia Wolfe, Jori Kandra, Lora Engdahl, and Heidi Shierholz, "Domestic Workers Chartbook: A Comprehensive Look at the Demographics, Wages, Benefits, and Poverty Rates of the Professionals Who Care for Our Family Members and Clean Our Homes," Economic Policy Institute, May 14, 2020, https://www.epi.org/publication/domestic-workers-chartbook-a-comprehensive-look-at-the-demographics-wages-benefits-and-poverty-rates-of-the-professionals-who-care-for-our-family-members-and-clean-our-homes/#:~:text=here

%20are%202.2%20million%20domestic,from%20illness%2C%20or
%20have%20disabilities.

17. Harney and Moten, *The Undercommons*, 74.

18. Michel Serres, *The Parasite*, trans. Lawrence R. Schehr (Minneapolis: Minnesota University Press, 1982), 2.

19. Burnham and Theodore, *Home Economics*.

20. Kathryn Yusoff, *A Billion Black Anthropocenes or None* (Minneapolis: University of Minnesota Press, 2019).

21. Aimé Césaire, *Return to My Native Land* (New York: Archipelago Books, 1969).

22. June Barrett, interview by Marisa Morán Jahn, Pérez Art Museum, Miami, January 14, 2017.

23. Erlinda Alvarez, interview by Marisa Morán Jahn, North Chicago, February 16, 2015.

Creation as Counterpower

Carehaus: Designing for Care

Marisa Morán Jahn and Rafi Segal

Home?

Globalization in the late twentieth century involved not only massive shifts in finance, transnational labor, and the concentration of wealth in cities but also the resulting restructuring of the domestic sphere. As women in industrialized countries continued to relocate en masse to workplaces in locations geographically farther away from their aging relatives' homes, dual income–earning households began relying on the labor of millions of domestic workers emigrating predominantly from the Global South to the Global North.[1] Within this new "curo-sphere,"[2] there emerged new patterns in the displacement of care and the restructuring of domestic labor.

Born in India, Mona was married in Nepal and afterward worked as a trekking guide. She speaks five languages fluently. The Maoist insurgency of 1996 left an already weakened Nepalese economy in a state of economic collapse. Mona, like thousands of others, scrambled to find work. Unable to feed her five- and six-year-old children, she immigrated to Queens, New York, to work as a nanny and send money home. While in the United States, she was misinformed about a visa filing requirement and ultimately resorted to working under the table. As an undocumented immigrant without legal protection, should Mona return to Nepal to visit her family, she might not be able to return to New York City to earn the essential wages on which her family back home relies. With that knowledge, she had to make a choice no parent should ever have to consider and decided to stay in the United States to function as her family's financial lifeline. While she regularly chats with her two daughters via WhatsApp, she has not hugged her daughters for seventeen years.[3] She works seven days a week to put her two daughters through college but will not be able to see them graduate.

Mona is among the 2.5 million other domestic workers in the United States employed as nannies, housekeepers, and caregivers.[4] Of the over two thousand domestic workers participating in a national survey in 2011–2012, more than 90 percent were women, 60 percent of their income went toward covering rent or mortgage payments, and an even higher percentage were paid below the state minimum wage.[5] "The money we earn here in the States does not go far—housing here in New York is so expensive! We live modestly so that we can send money home," explains Narbada Chhetri, a talented singer and community organizer at Adhikaar for Human Rights. Her words capture the shared sense of mutualism that runs high in her community to counter housing insecurity. "Sometimes I meet new immigrants from Nepal who have no place to go. It was like that for me too when I first came—and I want to help my sisters."[6]

When asked about her vision for the future, Narbada's voice starts to crack. She breaks into silent tears. "Many of us have lived in New York for over two decades. We've made a home with each other, and some of us have children who have grown up here. What will happen to us when we get older? My dream is to have a home where me and my sisters can live together when we are old."

Paradox of Care

Mona's and Narbada's stories embody the paradox of care across the United States and in other industrialized countries. On the one hand, domestic workers provide essential labor by ensuring our loved ones eat nutritious meals, attend medical appointments, take prescriptions, socialize, and stay healthy. But on the other hand, despite their roles as critical lifelines, caregivers in the United States are part of an industry characterized by low wages and high turnover. Working in isolation and with weak labor protections, caregivers disproportionately suffer from workplace injuries and sexual abuse on the job. While caregiving has been the United States' fastest-growing workforce, this growth is unable to keep pace with the aging baby boomer population and the smaller, dispersed families unable to care for aging and disabled individuals.[7]

This care deficit impacts individuals, families, and society at large. In 2016, the average time to fill an hourly wage job in caregiving was forty-two 42 days[8]—a critical gap during which older adults were unable to receive basic, daily care and often suffered preventable injuries or missed medication. These care deficits result in costly hospital visits internalized and paid for by patients, their insurance companies, or public taxpayers.[9]

A global housing shortage only compounds industrialized countries' care crises. In the United States, California alone requires an estimated 3.5 million new housing units—a shortage the state's governor hopes to remedy by 2050. According to the mortgage lender Freddie Mac, the United States must build an additional 370,000 homes a year to meet demand.[10] The unprecedented growth in the number of senior households will test the ability of the nation's housing stock to address the spiraling need for affordable, accessible, and supportive units.

Given the shortage of housing and those who can provide care, it's clear, then, that finding ways to mutualize both housing and care will be critical.

Change

In the past decade, labor policies in the United States have begun to catch up to recognize that increasing the stability of caregivers directly impacts the well-being of older and disabled people as well as working families. Driving this movement for change are women like Mona, Narbada, Marlene, and ten thousand other domestic workers and advocates from diverse cultures throughout the United States. Organized through the National Domestic Workers Alliance, this movement, led by immigrants and women, results in changing legislation granting domestic workers basic workplace rights. This vision of racial and economic justice for the United States' two million domestic workers[11] includes increasing living wages, strengthening workforce protections, and curbing abuse on the job.

Alongside critical policy shifts that can ideally scale along national lines, the United States needs bold solutions for how our urban environment can center and mutualize care. Aquilina Soriano-Versoza, executive director of the Los Angeles–based Pilipino Workers Center, frames this as a moral imperative: "We as a society have a responsibility to make sure that those who want to stay independent and have a good quality of life can get that care. But we also need to make sure that we are building jobs that are good, sustainable that people can raise their own families on." This means transforming our homes and cities to support what's referred to as congregate care (or group care). For example, right now, disproportionate workplace abuse occurs in the prevailing live-in model, wherein caregivers and their clients live together in isolation. Aquilina describes the significance of designing for social integration and with multiple caregivers:

> For caregivers, something that would really transform the industry is if we changed the live-in setup where you had more than one worker for situations that need around-the-clock care. The current live-in model sets people up to be treated as servants more than workers. And you know, it's hard to be a whole person as a live-in; they are there as a worker twenty-four hours a day; they are not able to be freely themselves, whereas time for socializing and whatever they want to do is important. So changing the live-in setup would be crucial.[12]

Alongside other innovations to enable mutualizing care, we have the opportunity to leverage the symbolic power of art, architecture, and design to inspire us to value care. According to Ai-jen Poo, director of the National Domestic Workers Alliance, "Art allows us to dream bigger, dream futures into being that we've never experienced and create new protagonists."[13] Consider that most of the celebrated buildings in our cities are devoted to well-endowed cultural institutions and wealthy corporations. We ask, What would it look like to build in celebration of care—specifically the labor of care? And more broadly, how might an architecture of care strengthen solidarity with care workers to transform our fractured "curo-scape"?[14]

Carehaus: A New Model for Living and Care

In response to the growing need for care solutions, we (artist Marisa Morán Jahn and architect Rafi Segal) joined forces with real estate developer and urban planner Ernst Valery to establish Carehaus, the United States' first care-based cohousing project.

Carehaus Baltimore designed by Rafi Segal in collaboration with Marisa Morán Jahn.

Founded by Jahn, Segal, and their third partner, Ernst Valery, Carehaus is the first care-based co-housing building in the United States. Carehaus provides quality care and homes for older and disabled adults as well as quality jobs and homes for caregivers and their families. The first location in Baltimore features twenty-one units, housing fifteen older adults and disabled people, five caregivers with their families, and a health/art residency.

Carehaus is a new type of residential building for older adults, disabled people, and caregivers and their families. Carehaus provides independent living units for all its residents, clustered around shared spaces that support shared meals, child care, and various other activities such as art, fitness, physical therapy, financial literacy courses, and horticulture in the open garden spaces. Combined with culturally relevant programs in partnership with local arts organizations, Carehaus's art initiatives aid in improving cognitive health and create a unique sense of place.

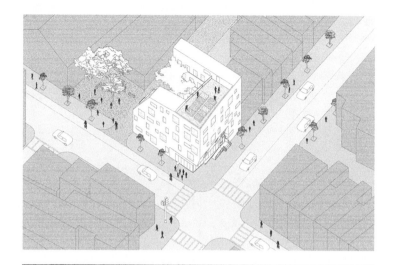

Located in the historically divested neighborhood of Johnston Square, *Carehaus Baltimore* is designed as a neighborhood anchor. Street-level retail, communal spaces, and art integrated into the façade activate the urban corner, contributing to the neighborhood's revitalization as an erstwhile cultural corridor.

Here's how Carehaus works: Older and disabled adults receive quality care and developmentally appropriate homes. In exchange for their labor, caregivers receive good wages, subsidized meals and housing, and other benefits.

Carehaus's design for congregate care or care sharing makes caregiving more efficient and safer: caregivers can take turns keeping an eye on those who need close monitoring or lend a hand to support tasks such as leaning over to lift residents.

In this coliving community, Carehaus residents share utilities, meals, appliances, and tools. By optimizing care and labor, energy consumption, and minimizing food waste,

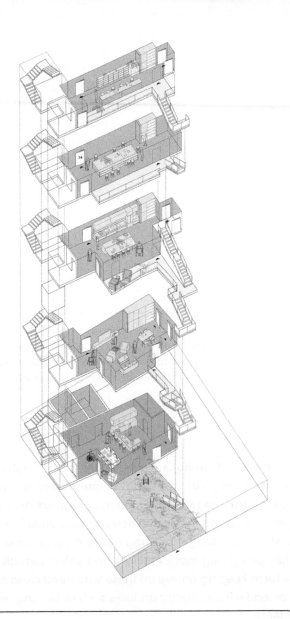

Carehaus Baltimore's shared spaces and courtyard-facing terraces support different communal activities (kitchen, lounge, work space, and others). These communal areas enable shared meals, pastimes, relaxation, gardening, art and fitness classes, shared caregiving, and more. Stairs and an elevator connect all the shared areas to allow ease of use and access for tenants.

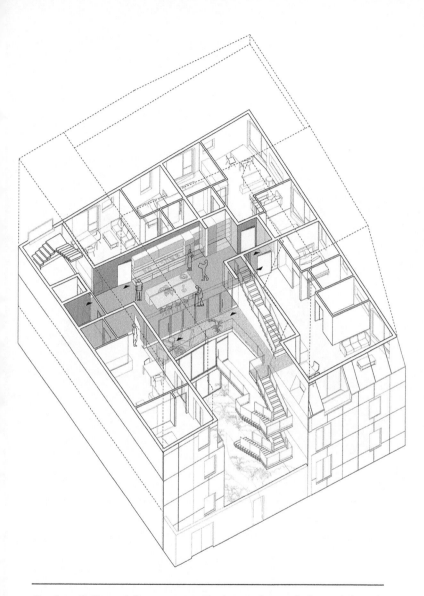

Carehaus Baltimore's floors are organized around centrally-located shared spaces. As seen in the third floor, a kitchen and an open terrace anchor a variety of residential units: studio, one-bedroom, and two-bedroom units, accommodating residents' varying household sizes. The abundance and ease of access to the shared space make caregiving more efficient and safer: caregivers can take turns keeping an eye on those who need close monitoring or support each other in tasks.

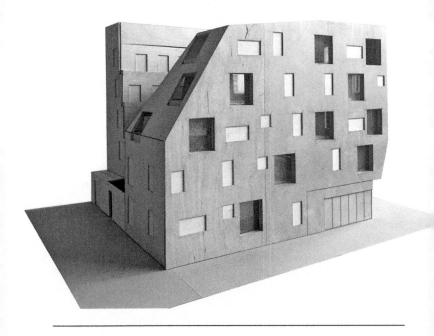

Carehaus model

Rafi Segal A+U, 2020

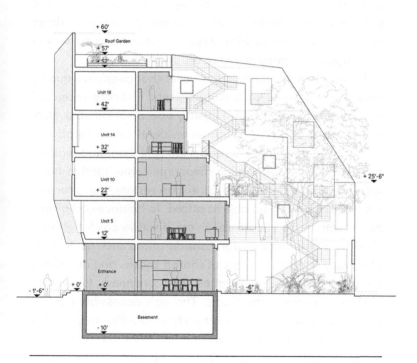

Carehaus Baltimore is a five-story building designed around a shared courtyard allowing ground-level access from both street and alley. This cross section through the courtyard shows how the floors set back sequentially to ensure better light and air circulation and allow interaction between the terraces and the shared courtyard

Carehaus is able to pass these cost savings on to residents in the form of benefits—higher-quality care for residents and sustainable wages for caregivers.

Drawing on historical examples of multigenerational collectives that have integrated care into their social and physical structure,[15] Carehaus is being developed as different building types in various scales: from the smallest set of floors in a high rise, to an individual residential building, to a set of buildings that occupy an entire urban block.

Carehaus is founded on the belief that consistent quality care requires centering both caregivers' and care-receivers' needs. By providing both housing and a sustainable work environment, Carehaus balances residents' needs for privacy with shared amenities, increases job retention, and reduces turnover. These cost-saving measures come hand in hand with more hours of quality care than resident care receivers would normally be able to afford. To balance caregivers' needs with those of care-receivers, iterative co-design sessions help determine design considerations such as degrees of privacy and security, use of shared spaces and amenities, caregiver to care-receiver ratios, child care needs, fair wages, and management structures. Through accessible design, communal programming, and architecture that responds to and celebrates its urban environment, Carehaus enables its residents: older adults and disabled people, and their caregivers to integrate into their community, empowered to fully participate in a democratic society.

Carehaus's first building is scheduled to be constructed in a historically divested neighborhood of Baltimore, Maryland. The five-story corner building of twenty units will house about fifteen older and/or disabled adults, five caregivers, and one additional residency that contribute to a communal art and health program. Carehaus Baltimore has been designed in response to the community's self-identified need to enrich

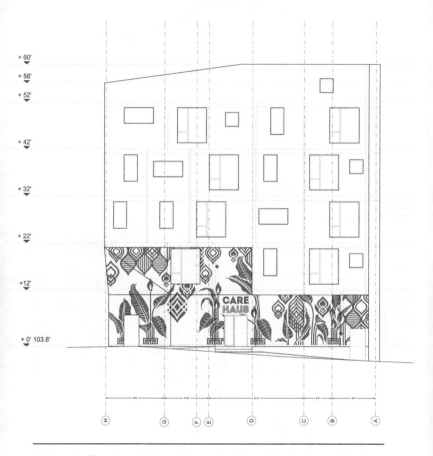

Meshworks (Carehaus Baltimore). Design by Marisa Morán Jahn; architecture by Rafi Segal, 2021.

The design of Carehaus's street level façade revisits the Baltimorean tradition of painted window screens, which allows residents to see the street while negotiating their privacy. Fabricated from perforated metal panels placed in front of colored, lit walls, the façade creates an urban-scale, jewel-box effect responding to the local residents' desire for an illuminated streetscape.

The façade's iconography integrates motifs of a peace lily—a symbol of hope, harmony, and new beginnings—expressing the neighbor's call to revive the area's former cultural legacy.

Stories of Solidarity, 2021. Design by Marisa Morán Jahn with Rafi Segal.

Integrating art into Carehaus activates cultural heritages, improves cognitive health, and fosters a unique sense of place. This installation at the Blaffer Art Museum transposes the designs for *Carehaus Baltimore's* first two floors

into a museum space in its real life-size scale. Photo courtesy of the Blaffer Art Museum and Cynthia Woods Mitchell Center for the Arts, University of Houston; Photo by Sean Fleming.

the streetscape through retail, community programs and activities, and social integration.

We are taking this approach to other sites and cities where Carehauses directly respond to the specific local needs of domestic workers, immigrant families, and those who need care. For example, some communities prioritize retail and streetscape activities as ways to stabilize the neighborhood, while other communities prioritize access to green space. Some communities may be well-served by an on-site health clinic for residents and surrounding neighbors, while others, located adjacent to existing medical facilities, may have different needs. Drawing on our team's experience in community organizing, dialogue between local stakeholders builds open pathways for ongoing communication and collaboration among stakeholders.

Founded on the belief that art and storytelling enable us to live our lives to the fullest and should be accessible at each stage of life, Carehaus integrates the arts into its DNA. Numerous studies have demonstrated the beneficial effects of arts programming and expressive arts[16] for older adults by reducing depression and anxiety symptomatic of chronic diseases, building new neural pathways and stronger dendrites to counter cognitive decline, and enhancing memory retention. Culturally relevant programs developed in partnership with local arts organizations enable Carehaus residents to activate, express, and pass on cultural heritages.

More fundamentally, we believe that art plays an essential role in identity formation and narrative building, helping to forge an understanding of self, inviting us to proudly identify as caregivers, care receivers, or those who will likely need care as we age. Without this already formed identity, architecture is hollow: it tarries in the hypothetical and operates in a void.

In insisting on the importance of art and architecture when redesigning the spatial conditions to support care equity,

As seen in this model of *Carehaus Baltimore*, each floor's wall mural features a distinct interior mural which enables wayfinding, memory-boxing, and sensory stimulation. This new design approach breaks from the typical institutional care facilities characterized by their uniformity and sterility. Model by Kader Haytham and Paul Gruber.

we take an *integrationist approach* to cultural production. We see ourselves responding to the challenges of our time, making art and architecture to shape new social realities. We are again in a moment of immense upheaval—a growing care crisis, an economic recovery in the wake of a global pandemic, and a national housing shortage. At the same time, we are in a period of renewed recognition of caregivers' essential labor. Given these unique challenges, we have the opportunity to embrace the role of art, architecture, and design to harness the power of mutualism that was always already ours.

Carehaus Team ⁓⁓⁓⁓⁓⁓⁓⁓⁓⁓⁓⁓⁓⁓⁓⁓⁓⁓⁓⁓⁓⁓⁓⁓⁓⁓⁓⁓⁓

Design: Rafi Segal A+U, collaborating artist Marisa Morán Jahn

Design team: Alina Nazmeeva, Paul Soren Gruber.

Research Team: Ana Paula Arenas, Adiel Benitez, Laura Cadena, Nina Huttenman, Noa Machover, Charlotte Rose Matthai, Alberto Luís Meouchi Velez, Ned Ohringer, Lesley Onstott, Ixchel Ramirez, Sarah Rege, Vaidehi Supatkar, Meghan Timmons, Marisa Concetta Waddle.

Notes

1. Rhacel Salazar Parreñas, *Servants of Globalization: Migration and Domestic Work*, 2nd ed. (Stanford, CA: Stanford University Press, 2015).
2. Hironori Onuki, "Care, Social (Re)production and Global Labour Migration: Japan's 'Special Gift' Toward 'Innately Gifted' Filipino Workers," *New Political Economy* 14, no. 4 (2009): 489–516, https://www.tandfonline.com/doi/abs/10.1080/13563460903287306.
3. Mona Lama, interview by Marisa Morán Jahn, Baltimore, September 21, 2015, and electronic correspondence.
4. The National Domestic Workers Alliance conservatively estimates this number to be two million; other sources have estimated that there are as many as five million domestic workers.
5. Linda Burnham and Nik Theodore, *Home Economics: The Invisible and Unregulated World of Domestic Work* (New York: National Domestic Workers Alliance, 2012), https://www.domesticworkers.org/wp-content/uploads/2021/06/HomeEconomicsReport.pdf.
6. Narbada Chhetri, interview by Marisa Morán Jahn, Adhikaar for Human Rights, Queens, New York, February 16, 2016.
7. Ari Medoff, interview by Anjum Asharia and Marc Shavitz, Durham, NC, Monday, March 13, 2017. Also see Mark Miller, "The Future of U.S. Caregiving: High Demand, Scarce Workers," Reuters, August 3, 2017, https://www.reuters.com/article/us-column-miller-caregivers/the-future-of-u-s-caregiving-high-demand-scarce-workers-idUSKBN1AJ1JQ.
8. Society for Human Resource Management, *2016 Human Capital Benchmarking Report* (Alexandria, VA: Society for Human Resource Management, 2016), 16, https://www.shrm.org/hr-today/trends-and-forecasting/research-and-surveys/pages/2016-human-capital-report.aspx.

Essays

Poster for *Carehaus Baltimore* illustrated by Marisa Morán Jahn, 2021.

9. In the state of Maryland, a single visit to the hospital costs between $8,000 and $15,000. See Tara Golshan, "The Answer to America's Health Care Cost Problem May Be in Maryland," Vox, January 22, 2020, https://www.vox.com/policy-and-politics/2020/1/22/21055118/maryland-health-care-global-hospital-budget.

10. Sam Khater, Len Kiefer, Ajita Atreya, and Venkataramana Yanamandra, *The Major Challenge of Inadequate U.S. Housing Supply* (McLean, VA: Federal Home Loan Mortgage Corporation [Freddie Mac], December 5, 2018), http://www.freddiemac.com/fmac-resources/research/pdf/201811-Insight-06.pdf.

11. This is a conservative statistic provided by the National Domestic Workers Alliance as of March 30, 2021.

12. Aquilina Soriano-Versoza, interview by Marisa Morán Jahn, Pilipino Worker Center, Los Angeles, March 12, 2014.

13. Ai-jen Poo, "CareForce: Creating a Future with Care Workers as Protagonists," Visible, accessed March 25, 2021, https://www.visibleproject.org/blog/text/careforce-creating-a-future-with-care-workers-as-protagonists/.

14. Onuki, "Care, Social (Re)production and Global Labour Migration."

15. Among the many case studies worth noting, the movement led by a nineteenth-century material feminist to transform the spatial conditions of the domestic sphere in North America continues to inspire.

Starting in the United States in the mid-1800s, feminist reformers and designers such as Melusina Fay Peirce, Marie Stevens Howland, Mary Livermore, Ellen Swallow Richards, and Charlotte Perkins Gilman designed collectivist homes with the goal of mutualizing domestic labor and in turn achieving political emancipation and economic justice. As historian Dolores Hayden writes,

> Material feminists expounded one powerful idea: that women must create feminist homes with socialized housework and child care before they could become truly equal members of society. . . . [These women] argued that the entire physical environment of cities and towns must be redesigned to reflect equality for women. (*The Grand Domestic Revolution: A History of Feminist Designs for American Homes, Neighborhoods, and Cities* [Cambridge, MA: MIT Press, 1981], 3, 8).

During this movement's most active period, thousands of families on the East Coast lived in these communitarian homes, where meals, care, and housework were shared. From this often-overlooked period in North American history, one important takeaway is the missed opportunity for nineteenth-century materialists to build solidarity among middle- and working-class women. Today, with the growing recognition that consistent, quality care for care receivers is directly tied to the socioeconomic welfare of caregivers, it's clear that designs *must* center the needs of both stakeholder groups.

16. Barbara Bagan, "What's Art Got to Do with It?," *Today's Geriatric Medicine*, accessed March 27, 2021, https://www.todaysgeriatricmedicine.com/news/ex_082809_03.shtml.

Acknowledgments

Many thanks to our literary agent, Joan Brookbank; to our generous thought partners, Greg Lindsay, Amy Rosenblum-Martín, and Koray Caliskan; and to our contributors.

Research support: Alina Nazmeeva, Laura Cadena, Mengfu Kuo, Ben Segal, Juhi Sharma, Vernon Rudolph, Marc Shavitz, Anjum Asharia.

This book was supported by a grant from the Graham Foundation for Advanced Studies in the Fine Arts.

About the Authors and Contributors

The Authors

Rafi Segal is an architect and associate professor of architecture and urbanism at the Massachusetts Institute of Technology. His work involves design and research on the architectural, urban, and regional scales, currently focused on how emerging notions of collectivity can impact the design of buildings and cities. His ongoing work includes designs for new communal neighborhoods in Israel, Rwanda, and the Philippines. Segal directs Future Urban Collectives, a new design-research lab at MIT that explores the relation between digital platforms and physical communities, asking how architecture and urbanism can support and scale cohabitation, coproduction, and coexistence. He has exhibited his work at venues including the Storefront for Art and Architecture, NYC; KunstWerk, Berlin; Witte de With, Rotterdam; Venice Biennale of Architecture; Museum of Modern Art, NYC; and Hong Kong/Shenzhen Urbanism Biennale. He holds a PhD from Princeton University and a MSc and a BArch from Technion, Israel Institute of Technology. rafisegal.com.

Marisa Morán Jahn's art and films redistribute power, "exemplifying the possibilities of art as social practice" (ArtForum). Codesigned with youth, new immigrants, and working families, Jahn's work has engaged millions through venues such as the Tribeca Film Festival, Obama's White House, the United Nations, PBS, The New York Times, CNN, the BBC, Univision Global, the Museum of Modern Art, and the Venice Biennale of Architecture. Her key works include Bibliobandido, a story-eating bandit whose fame in Honduras rivals Santa Claus; two mobile studios (NannyVan, CareForce One) and a Sundance-supported PBS film amplifying the voices of caregivers; and Carehaus, the U.S.'s first care-based co-housing project designed with architect Rafi Segal. She has taught at Teachers College at Columbia University, Massachusetts Institute of Technology (her alma mater), and Parsons/The New School where she is the Director of Integrated Design. In 2022, she is a Sundance Fellow, an Artist/Writer in Residence at the Brooklyn Public Library, and a Senior Researcher at MIT. marisajahn.com

The Contributors

Mercedes Bidart, born and raised in Argentina, is dedicated to creating innovative pathways for economic justice. She founded Quipu, a digital platform that supports shared wealth generation in low-income, informal economies. Her work has been featured in *Forbes*, *Norman Foster Foundation Stories*, and *El País*, and she has received awards from the MIT Innovation Initiative, MIT DesignX Accelerator, Google.org, Fast Forward Accelerator, World Bank Youth Summit, and IDB Lab, among others. She holds a master's degree from the Massachusetts Institute of Technology (Fulbright Scholar) and a bachelor in political science from the University of Buenos Aires. Before MIT, she worked for five years in the Cities Program of CIPPEC, a Latin American think tank, where she did research and knowledge exchange among local governments.

Arturo Escobar is an activist-researcher from Cali, Colombia, working on territorial struggles against extractivism, postdevelopmentalist and postcapitalist transitions, and ontological design. He was a professor of anthropology and political ecology at the University of North Carolina, Chapel Hill, until 2018 and is currently affiliated with PhD programs in design and creation (University of Caldas, Manizales, Colombia) and in environmental sciences (University of Valle, Cali). Over the past twenty-five years, he has worked closely with Afrodescendant, environmental, and feminist organizations in Colombia. His most well-known book is *Encountering Development: The Making and Unmaking of the Third* World (1995; 2nd ed. 2011). His most recent books are *Designs for the Pluriverse: Radical Interdependence, Autonomy, and the Making of Worlds* (2018) and *Pluriversal Politics: The Real and the Possible* (2020).

Jessica Gordon Nembhard, PhD, is a political economist and chair of the Department of Africana Studies at John Jay College, City University of New York, where she is a professor of community justice and social economic development. She has written numerous publications on cooperative economics, community economic development, credit unions, wealth inequality, community wealth, and black political economy. She is the author of *Collective Courage: A History of African American Cooperative Economic Thought and Practice* (2014) and a 2016 inductee into the U.S. Cooperative Hall of Fame.

Michael Hardt, a political philosopher and literary theorist, is best known for three books he coauthored with Antonio Negri: *Empire* (2000), *Multitude: War and Democracy in the Age of Empire* (2004), and *Commonwealth* (2009). The trilogy—and, in particular, its first volume, *Empire*—has often been hailed as the "Communist Manifesto of the 21st century." Hardt is a professor of literature at Duke University and a professor of philosophy at the European Graduate School.

Greg Lindsay is the director of applied research at the NewCities Foundation and director of strategy at its mobility offshoot, CoMotion. He is also a nonresident senior fellow of the Atlantic Council's Foresight, Strategy, and Risks Initiative; a senior fellow of MIT Architecture's Future Urban Collectives Lab; and a partner at FutureMap, a geo-strategic advisory firm based in Singapore. His writing and research on the future of cities, work, and organizations has been published in the *New York Times*, *Harvard Business Review*, *Time*, *Wired*, *Fast Company*, *New Republic*, and many other publications. His work with Studio Gang Architects on the future of suburbia was displayed at New York's Museum of Modern Art in 2012. His work has also been displayed at the 15th, 16th, and 17th Venice Architecture Biennales, the International Architecture Biennale Rotterdam, and Habitat III. He was guest curator of the 2018 and 2019 editions of the reSITE festival in Prague.

Ai-jen Poo is the cofounder and executive director of the National Domestic Workers Alliance (NDWA), a nonprofit organization working to achieve respect, recognition, and fairness for domestic workers, the majority of whom are immigrants and women of color. Under her leadership, the NDWA has helped to pass a Domestic Workers' Bill of Rights in ten states and the cities of Seattle and Philadelphia and has brought more than two million home-care workers under minimum wage protections. She is the author of *The Age of Dignity: Preparing for the Elder Boom in a Changing America* (2015), a book that helps Americans reflect on the needs of and opportunities in the elder boom in order to improve access to care for all families while ensuring a strong care workforce for the future. In 2019, she also cofounded SuperMajority, a new home for women's activism, that trains and mobilizes a multiracial, intergenerational community to fight for gender and racial equity. Poo is a 2014 MacArthur Fellow and a TIME 100 alumna and has been named by *Fortune* as one of the world's fifty greatest leaders. Her work has appeared in the *New York Times*, *Washington Post*, and *Time* and at CNN.com, among others. She currently serves as a trustee of the Ford Foundation and a member of the Democratic National Committee.

Index

Page numbers in *italics* indicate illustrations.

adversarial design, 171

affordable housing: housing shortage and, 185; in Rwanda, *8–10, 142–147*

Airbnb, 78, 130

Airtable, 88, 97

A La Carte, 170

Alia, 116

alternative economies, 15

Altman, Irwin, 129

Alvarez, Erlinda, 17–18, 20–21, 177

Amancay, 102

Anti-Defamation League, 25n4

Arabian Nights, 14

architecture, 2; capitalism and, 128; of caregiving, 187; of Carehaus, 193, 198–199; for collective housing, 127–136, *137–153*; in Covid-19 pandemic, 128; for domestic workers, 25; gig economy and, 128; implementation requirements of, 4–5; for new collectives, 127–136, *137–153*; space and, 127; of undercommons, 174

art: on *A La Carte*, 170; at Carehaus, 188, *196–197*, 198–199, *199*; for commons, 122–123; for domestic workers, 25; kits for, 170–171; solidarity from, 187. *See also* public art

Asharia, Anjum, 25n3, 157

Astoria Mutual Aid, in New York City, 89

autonomy: with capitalism, 54; transition design and, 48. *See also* self-determination

Baltimore. *See* Carehaus

Barrett, June, 177

Bataille, Georges, 168–169

bayanihan, 15

B Corp movement, 70

Bed-Stuy Strong, 89

Belgium, 84

Bibliobandido (Story Eater), 11–14, *12, 13,* 26n6

Bidart, Mercedes, 24–25; on Quipu, 99–111

Biden, Joe, 119

Billion Black Anthropocenes or None, A (Yusoff), 27n19

biodesign, 49

biophilic urbanism, 49

BIPOC: people of color, monuments to, 4; solidarity with, 23. *See also* women of color

Black Communities' Process (Proceso de Comunidades Negras, PCN), 41

Black Lives Matter, 165; solidarity and, 63

Black Panther Party, 87, 97
Blacks: as caregivers, 164; co-ops of, 65–68; as domestic workers, 163; Historically Black Colleges and Universities for, 11; as housekeepers, 164; mutual aid societies of, 60, 65–68; Underground Railroad and, 58–59
Bloomberg, Michael, *3*
Bolden, Dorothy, 165
Bollier, David, 54
Bologna, Italy, bike delivery system in, 82–83
Boroughs, Nannie Helen, 64
Boston, Brazilian Worker Center in, 167–168
bottom-up movements, 7; for China's Covid-19 pandemic response, 88–89; for disaster relief, 87; for domestic workers, 163
Brazil, 34; cooperatives in, 74; transportation cooperatives in, 76
Brazilian Worker Center, in Boston, 167–168
brick, in Rwanda, 7, *10*
Brigade Network, 92
Brightly Cleaning Cooperative, 76
Britain: home-care cooperative in, 79; unionized worker cooperatives in, 81
Build Back Better, 119
buildings, 1; individualism and, 50; in new collectives, 135; space and, 127; in Underground Railroad, 59

built environment: individualism and, 50; interdependence and, 49; in Quipu, 104, 111
Buttigieg, Pete, 94
Byatt, A. S., 14

California: Domestic Workers' Bill of Rights of, *172*; housing shortage in, 185
Cantave, Glenn, 4
capitalism: architecture and, 128; autonomy with, 54; caregiving and, 17; commons and, 31, 54; community-centered economies with, 21–22; cooperatives and, 84; feminism and, 53; GDP in, 21; mutualism and, 15–16; patriarchy and, 35–36; transition design and, 53; in United States, 53
care banks, 15
Careforce Disco, 172
CareForce: laughter with, 168–169; public art project by, *19*
CareForce One, 5–6, 161, *161*, *178*, 179
caregivers/caregiving: architecture of, 187; average time to fill job in, 185; Blacks as, 164; at Carehaus, 189, 194; challenges of, 114–115; child care for, 120; as commons, 121–123; in Covid-19 pandemic, 25, 116–119, 122; crisis of, in United States, 113–123, 185; devaluing of, 120; as essential workers, 116–117; housing shortage and, 185–186; in Hurricane

Sandy, 117–118; inequality in, 120–121; infrastructure for, 119–120, 122; live-in model for, 186–187; by millennials, 113–114; mutualism and, 113–123; paid sick days for, 118; paradox of, 184–185; public art project for, *19*; raise the floor for, 119–120; sexual harassment of, 185; socioeconomic justice for, 17; turnover of, 115, 185; in United States, 160; by women of color, 17, 27n19. *See also* nannies

Carehaus, 6, *20*, 64–68, 183–199, *189*; architecture of, 193, 198–199; art at, *196–197*, 198–199, *199*; caregivers at, 189, 194; in Covid-19 pandemic, 135, 199; culture at, 198–199; design of, *195*; model of, *192*; as new collective, 134–135; poster for, *201*; privacy at, 194; shared spaces in, *190*, *191*, *193*, 194; storytelling at, 198

Caring Across Generations, 25, 116, 163; CareForce One and, *161*

Carnegie Mellon, School of Design of, 53

cartel law, in United States, 77

Castellanos, Guillermina: NannyVan and, 25n3; *Voices from the CareForce* and, *173*

Césaire, Suzanne, 166, 177

Champion, Marlene, 160

Chesapeake Marine Railway and Dry Dock Company, 66

Chhetri, Narbada, 184; NannyVan and, 25n3; *Voices from the CareForce* and, *173*

child care: for caregivers, 120; at Carehaus, 188; rising costs of, *162*

China, Covid-19 pandemic in, 88–89

Coalition for Human Rights Los Angeles (CHRLA), *172*

Code of America, 91–93, 97

collective housing (co-housing), *7*, *20*; architecture for, 127–136, *137–153*; at Carehaus, 6; feminism for, 202n15; *maloca*, 51–53, *52*; sharing economy and, 130–131. *See also* Carehaus

collective neighborhoods, in Rwanda, *7*

collectives: cooperatives and, 69–71. *See also* new collectives

Columbia: liberation of Mother Earth in, 49; PCN in, 41; transition design in, 53. *See also* Quipu

Common Ground Relief, for Hurricane Katrina, 87

common pool resources (CPRs), 15

commons: capitalism and, 31, 54; caregiving as, 121–123; categories of, 31–32; culture and, 122–123; defined, 2, 31–32; democracy and, 32–33; design of, 31–33; discussion on, 31–39; scale and, 33–37; sharing economy and, 37–39; solidarity and, 33–37

communism, 16

community-centered economies, 17; with capitalism, 21–22

contagion, of social movements, 34

Cooperative Digital Economy, at
The New School, 24
cooperatives (co-ops), 16–17;
created by Black communities,
60–61, 65–68; in Brazil, 74;
capitalism and, 84; collectives
and, 69–71; competitive
advantages of, 73–74, 79; in
crises, 62–63; democracy in,
80–81; design for, 85–86; for-
profit businesses and, 72–73;
in France, 74; in gig economy,
78–79; governance in, 80–81;
government regulation of,
76–78; government support
for, 61–62; impact of, 67–68,
75–76; in Indonesia, 79; in Italy,
76–77; in Japan, 79; labor and,
69–86; local economic benefits
of, 26n13; low failure rates of,
26n11; misogyny in, 79, 85;
political tendencies of, 74–75;
privacy in, 73; replication
of, 76; Rochdale Society of
Equitable Pioneers, *71*; scale of,
75–76; social movements and,
84–85; trust in, 60; in United
States, 74, 76, 77; venture
capital model and, 79; women
in, 64, 73–74. *See also* platform
cooperatives; unionized
worker cooperatives
Costanza-Chock, Sasha, 166
Couchsurfing, 130
counterpower: creation as,
157–179; design of, 171–175;
for domestic workers, 115–116;
social movements and, 164–171
Covid-19 pandemic: architecture
in, 128; caregiving in, 25,
116–119, 122; Carehaus in,
135, 199; co-ops in, 16, 62;
domestic workers in, 160;
economic precarity in, 23;
mutual aid societies in, 87–91,
93, 128; mutualism in, 15, 24,
38; platform cooperatives in,
81–83; sharing economies in,
38; transition design and, 54
CPRs. *See* common pool
resources
creation, as counterpower,
157–179
crises: of caregiving, in United
States, 113–123; co-ops in,
62–63; defuturing in, 46;
mutual aid societies in, 62–63;
mutualism in, 15. *See also*
Covid-19 pandemic
culture: architecture and,
6; at Carehaus, 198–199;
commons and, 122–123; in new
collectives, 136

decolonization, 48–49
Defuturing (Fry), 46
defuturing, in design, 46
democracy, 1; commons and,
32–33; in cooperatives, 80–81;
corruption of term, 38–39; in
design, 37; individualism and,
50; in platform cooperatives,
69; transition design and, 48
Denmark, cooperatives in, 70
Department of Agrarian Reform,
in the Philippines, 17, 20
Department of Commerce, U.S.,
61
Department of Labor, U.S., 6
depatriarchization, 48–49

deracialization, 48–49

design: of Carehaus, *195*; of commons, 31–33; for cooperatives, 85–86; of counterpower, 171–175; defined, 2; defuturing in, 46; democracy in, 37; as dialogue, 22–25; for mutualism, 85–86; of new collectives, 132–136; for pluriverse, 23; for Quipu, 102, 104–105. *See also specific types*

digital-first organizing, mutual aid societies and, 87–98

digital platforms, in informal economies, 99–111

DiSalvo, Carl, 171

domestic workers, 5–6; Blacks as, 163; bottom-up movements for, 163; change for, 186–187; counterpower for, 115–116, 164–171; in Covid-19 pandemic, 160; emancipation of, 202n15; feminism for, 202n15; as frontline workers, 160; gig economy and, 123; globalization and, 183; Jahn and, 57; in marginalized communities, 163; NannyVan for, 157–177, *158–159*, *160*; number of, 171, 200n4; Occupational Safety and Health Administration and, 177; power over, 164–165; social movements of, 169–170; in United States, 5, 171; women as, 165–166. *See also* caregivers; housekeepers; nannies; National Domestic Workers Alliance

Domestic Workers' Bill of Rights: in California, *172*; in New York, 121, 166

Domestic Workers United, 166

DREAMer, 6, 25n4

driver co-op rideshare platform, in New York City, 82

Du Bois, W. E. B., 65

dugnat, 15

earth: commons of, 31–32; Covid-19 pandemic and, 54; reintegration of, 49

ecological design, 49

Egypt, 34

emancipation: of domestic workers, 202n15; land and, 58; solidarity and, 57–68; space and, 58

Emancipation Proclamation, 65

Escobar, Arturo, 21; on self-determination, 41–55

essential workers, caregivers as, 116–117

Essential Workers' Bill of Rights, 117

Facebook, 72, 73, 90–91, 97

Fair Labor Standards Act of 1938, 79

Federici, Silvia, 14

feminism: capitalism and, 53; for collective housing, 202n15; for domestic workers, 202n15; in United States, 35

financial literacy: at Carehaus, 66, 188; at Quipu, 108

Finland: *dugnat* in, 15; platform cooperatives in, 83

Floyd, George, 94, 98

FMSD. *See* Fundación Mario Santo Domingo
for-profit businesses, cooperatives and, 72–73
France, unionized worker cooperatives in, 74
freedom: corruption of term, 38–39; private property and, 128
Fricker, Miranda, 163
Fry, Tony, 46
Fundación Mario Santo Domingo (FMSD), 103

Garza, Alicia, 165
GDP, in capitalism, 21
genocidal leader monuments, replacement of, 4
Germany: cooperatives in, 70; Russia and, 35; venture capital model in, 77
Gibson-Graham, J. K., 2, 17, 21
gig economy, 23; architecture and, 128; cooperatives in, 78–79; domestic workers and, 123; inequalities of, 24; millennials in, 113; platform cooperatives and, 83
Gilets Jaunes, 34
Gillibrand (Senator), 77
Gilman, Charlotte Perkins, 202n15
globalization, 46; domestic workers and, 183; recommunalization from, 47; relocalization from, 48
Goldman, Emma, 84–85
Google docs, 87–88, 91
governance: in cooperatives, 80–81. *See also* democracy
gradient spaces, 155n16

Great Recession: co-ops in, 62; millennials and, 113
Greece, 34

Hardt, Michael, 23, 128, 168; on commons, 31–39
Harney, Stefano, 164, 174
Hayden, Dolores, 1–3, 130
Helfrich, Silke, 54
Heyworth, Charles, *71*
Historically Black Colleges and Universities, 11
Hoffelt, Stephany, 90–98
home-care cooperative, in Britain, 79
Honduras, literacy in, 11–14, *12*, *13*, 26n6
Hong Kong, 34
horizontal meshworks, 49
Horowitz, Sara, 11–12
Horowski, Meredith, 91–93, 97
housekeepers: Blacks as, 164; socioeconomic justice for, 17; in United States, 160
housing shortage, 185–186, 199
Howland, Marie Stevens, 202n15
Huang, Carmela, 166
Hurricane Katrina, 87
Hurricane Sandy: caregiving/caregivers in, 117–118; Occupy Sandy for, 87, 97
Hutton, Monica, *142*
hyperprivatization, 131

IDEPSCA. *See* Institute of Popular Education of Southern California
immigrants: solidarity with, 23; women of color, 5
Indignados, 33

individualism: in collective housing, 130; in new collectives, 132; in pluriverse, 49–51

Indonesia, cooperatives in, 79

inequality, 14; in caregiving, 120–121; transition design and, 53

informal economies: digital platforms in, 99–111; public housing and, 107–108; scale of, 108–109. *See also* Quipu

informal networks, 15

infrastructure: for caregiving, 119–120, 122; collapse of, mutual aid societies and, 7; of public housing, 110–111

Institute of Popular Education of Southern California (IDEPSCA), 166

integrated object, in new collectives, 135

interrogative design, 171

Iowa City Mutual Aid, 90–98

Israel: National Library of Israel, 135, *150–153*. *See also* kibbutz communities

Italy: Bologna, bike delivery system in, 82–83; cooperatives in, *76–77*; unionized worker cooperatives in, 74

Jahn, Marisa Morán, 5, *12*, *13*, *165*; on care and mutualism, 113–123; on commons, 31–39; on labor and co-ops, 69–86; public art project by, *19*; on Quipu, 99–111; on self-determination, 41–55; on solidarity and emancipation, 57–68; *Voices from the CareForce* and, *173*. *See also* CareForce; CareForce One; Carehaus; NannyVan

Japan, cooperatives in, 79

Jenkins, Henry, 169

Jorritsma, Marijke, *173*

Kerala, India, platform cooperatives in, 78, 82

Khullar, Dhruv, 17

kibbutz communities, 7; New Kibbutz, *137*; Segal and, 57

Kibbutz Hatzor, *138–141*

kits, in and as art, 170–171

Krawcheck, Anya, 157; NannyVan and, 25n3; *Voices from the CareForce* and, *173*

Kropotkin, Peter, 87

labor, co-ops and, 69–86

land: emancipation and, 58; in Quipu, 110–111

Lang, Jon, 129–130

Last Mile, 88–97

laughter, with CareForce One, 168–169

Leventhal Center for Advanced Urbanism (LCAU), at MIT, 103

Lewis, Christine, 25n3

LGBTQIA2S+, monuments to, 4

Lindsay, Greg, 24

literacy: in Honduras, 11–14, *12*, *13*, 26n6. *See also* financial literacy

Livermore, Mary, 202n15

Loconomics, 72–73

long-term care insurance, 113

Love Home Swap, 130

Luxemburg, Rosa, 35

Lyft, 78, 82
Lynch-Lloyd, Mary, *142*

maloca, 51–53, *52*
marginalized communities, 5;
    domestic workers in, 163
Medicaid, 113
Mexico, Zapatista movement of,
    46–47
millennials: caregiving by, 113–114;
    in gig economy, 113; in platform
    cooperatives, 79–80
misogyny, 35; in cooperatives,
    79, 85
MIT: Leventhal Center for
    Advanced Urbanism (LCAU)
    at, 103; Rwanda and, 7, *8–10,
    142–147*
Moten, Fred, 164, 174
Movers and Shakers, 4
multigenerational collectives, 193
multiplicity: differently designed
    worlds and, 47–48; of social
    movements, 34–37; solidarity
    and, 35–36
Multitude (Hardt and Negri), 31
mutual aid societies: in Baltimore,
    64–68; of Blacks, 60, 65–68;
    in Covid-19 pandemic, 87–91,
    93, 128; in crises, 62–63;
    digital-first organizing and,
    87–98; impact of, 67–68;
    infrastructural collapse and, 7;
    structural resilience of, 11; trust
    in, 60
mutualism: capitalism and,
    15–16; caregiving and, 113–123;
    in Covid-19 pandemic, 24,
    38; in crises, 15; defined, 2;
    design for, 85–86; housing

shortage and, 186; needs of,
    3–4; neoliberal privatization
    and, 14; in new collectives,
    131; in pluri-economies, 22; in
    social movements, 11, 14; of
    Underground Railroad, 24

nannies: in New York City, 183–184;
    socioeconomic justice for, 17; in
    United States, 160
NannyVan, 5–6, 25n3, 157–177,
    158–159; break down of, 177–
    179; pop-ups by, *160*, 174–175;
    space and, 174; Toddler Story
    Time Hour of, 170–171; trust in,
    169
"Nanthem," 175, 176–177
National Domestic Workers
    Alliance (NDWA), 5–6, 114, 163,
    186; affiliate organizations
    of, 116; CareForce One and,
    161; NannyVan and, 25n3; on
    number of domestic workers,
    200n4; Poo of, 17, 25, 187;
    public art project by, *19*
National Library of Israel, 135,
    150–153
NDWA. *See* National Domestic
    Workers Alliance
Negri, Antonio, 31, 128, 168
Neighborhood Express, 95
Nembhard, Jessica Gordon,
    16, 23–24, 26n11, 26n13; on
    solidarity and emancipation,
    57–68
Nepal, 183–184
nets *(redes)*, 23, 41–45, 54
new collectives: architecture for,
    127–136, *137–153*; buildings
    in, 135; culture in, 136; design

of, 132–136; individualism in, 132; integrated object in, 135; mutualism in, 131; nonuniform repetition for, 136; power in, 131; privacy in, 133; scale for, 132; space for, 132, 133; spatial gradient for, 134–135; user engagement in, 135–136

New Deal, 163; co-ops and, 61

New School, The, Cooperative Digital Economy at, 24

New York, Domestic Workers' Bill of Rights in, 121, 166

New York City: Astoria Mutual Aid in, 89; Bed-Stuy Strong in, 89; driver co-op rideshare platform in, 82; nannies in, 183–184

New Zealand, platform cooperatives in, 83

Next Kibbutz, *137*

Ngan, Ching Ying, *142*

nonuniform repetition, for new collectives, 136

Nucera, Diana, *173*

nuclear family, 3; displacement of, 127; in United States, 154n1

Occupational Safety and Health Administration, 177

Occupy Sandy, 87, 97

Occupy Wall Street, 34, 85

1001 Nights, 166

OntoShift, 54

Open Collectives, 47

open-source design: in platform cooperatives, 69; for Voz Mob, 166

ownership: of land, 58; in platform cooperatives, 70–71;

in Quipu, 110–111; short-term housing rentals and, 130; of suburban homes, 51; in United States, 154n3. *See also* private property

paid sick days, for caregivers, 118

Parks, Rosa, 165

Parvulescu, Anca, 169

patriarchy: capitalism and, 35–36; depatriarchization of, 48–49

PCN. *See* Proceso de Comunidades Negras (Black Communities' Process, PCN)

Peirce, Melusina Fay, 202n15

personal space, 129–130

Philippines, the: *bayanihan* in, 15; Department of Agrarian Reform in, 17, 20

Pilipino Workers Center, 186

platform cooperatives, 15, 69–75; in Covid-19 pandemic, 81–83; gig economy and, 83; in Kerala, India, 78, 82; millennials in, 79–80; open-source design in, 69; ownership in, 70–71; revolution and, 84–85; tenets of, 69

pluri-economies, 22

pluriverse, 21; design for, 23; differently designed worlds in, 47–48; individualism in, 49–51; transition design in, 45–46

Poo, Ai-jen, 17, 25, *165*, 187; on care and mutualism, 113–123; domestic workers and, 166; NannyVan and, 25n3

pop-ups, 4; for domestic workers, 5; by NannyVan, *160*, 174–175

postdevelopment theory, 51

power: control of, *47*; in
  new collectives, 131; over
  domestic workers, 164–165;
  re-constellation of, 22–23; of
  undercommons, 174. *See also*
  counterpower
Pradhan, Namrata, 25n3
privacy: at Carehaus, 194; in
  cooperatives, 73; defined, 129;
  government regulation of,
  165; in Kibbutz Hatzor, *139*; in
  new collectives, 133; in Next
  Kubbutz, *137*; private property
  and, 129; in Rwanda, *7*; senses
  involved in, 154n7; in space, 129
private property: commons
  and, 31; freedom and, 128;
  individualism and, 50; privacy
  and, 129; in United States, 128
Proceso de Comunidades Negras
  (Black Communities' Process,
  PCN), 41
public art: for caregiving, *19*; by
  Jahn, 57
public housing: informal
  economies and, 107–108;
  infrastructure of, 110–111

Quipu: built environment in, 104,
  111; in Columbia, 24–25, 99–111;
  credit score for, 101; design for,
  102, 104–105; discussion on,
  99–123; land in, 110–111; origin
  of, 102–103; ownership in,
  110–111; self-determination in,
  111; solidarity in, 102; space in,
  148, 149; tokens of, 100–101

racial harassment, in gig
  economy, 79

Ramirez, Vero, 176–177
recommunalization, from
  globalization, 47
redes (nets), 23, 41–45, 54
relocalization: from globalization,
  48; Quipu and, 99
revolution, platform cooperatives
  and, 84–85
Richards, Ellen Swallow, 202n15
Rochdale Society of Equitable
  Pioneers, *71*
Rodriguez, Daniel, 6
Rosales, Meches, 25n3
Russia, 35
Rwanda: affordable housing in,
  8–10, 142–147; brick in, *7, 10*;
  collective neighborhoods in, 7

scale: commons and, 33–37;
  of cooperatives, 75–76; of
  informal economies, 108–109;
  for new collectives, 132
Scheherazade (fictional
  character), 166
Schneider, Nathan, 11–12, 16–17
Scholtz, Trebor, 24; on labor and
  co-ops, 69–86
School of Design, of Carnegie
  Mellon, 53
seed banks, 15
Segal, Rafi, 6–7, *8–10*; on
  commons, 31–39; on labor
  and co-ops, 69–86; on Quipu,
  99–111; in Rwanda, *142–147*; on
  self-determination, 41–55; on
  solidarity and emancipation,
  57–68. *See also* Carehaus
self-determination, 1; discussion
  on, 41–55; in Quipu, 111
self-organizing meshworks, 49

self-study, in black coo-ops, 66–67

Serres, Michel, 176

sexual harassment: of caregivers, 185; of domestic workers, 164–165; in gig economy, 79

Shada, Steve, 170; NannyVan and, 25n3

sharing economy: collective housing and, 130–131; commons and, 37–39

Shavitz, Marc, 19; NannyVan and, 25n3

Shin, Taeseop, 142

Shopova, Maya, 142

short-term housing rentals, 76; ownership and, 130. See also Airbnb

Sievert, Jules Rochielle, 25n3

Signal, 97

Slack channels, 87–88, 97

social movements: contagion of, 34; cooperatives and, 84–85; counterpower and, 164–171; of domestic workers, 169–170; multiplicity of, 34–37; mutualism in, 11, 14; scale of, 33

solidarity: from art, 187; with BIPOC, 23; Black Lives Matter and, 63; commons and, 33–37; defined, 2; emancipation and, 57–68; with immigrants, 23; multiplicity and, 35–36; in Quipu, 102; of Underground Railroad, 24, 58–59, 59

Soriano-Versoza, Aquilina, 173, 186

South Africa, cooperatives in, 73, 85

space: architecture and, 127; emancipation and, 58; in Kibbutz Hatzor, 139; NannyVan and, 174; for new collectives, 132, 133; in Next Kubbutz, 137; personal, 129–130; pop-ups and, 175; privacy in, 129; in Quipu, 148, 149; territorialization of, 129–130; for Underground Railroad, 59

Spade, Dean, 11–12

Spain, 34; Indignados in, 33

spatial gradient: for new collectives, 134–135; in Next Kubbutz, 137

spreadability, 169

Staback, Danniely, 142

Stocksy, 75

Story Eater (Bibliobandido), 11–14, 12, 13, 26n6

storytelling: at Carehaus, 198; for commons, 122–123; for domestic workers, 25

structural resilience, 11

Sweden, cooperatives in, 70

TECHO, 102

territorialization, of space, 129–130

Territories of Difference (Escobar), 41

TEXT4BABY, 167

time banks, 15

Toddler Story Time Hour, 170–171

topo-digital, 131

Tracy, Natalicia, 25n3

transition design, 45–47; urgency of, 53–55

transportation cooperatives, in Brazil, 76

trust: in co-ops, 60; in mutual aid societies, 60; in NannyVan, 169

Tunisia, 34
Turkey, 34
turnover, of caregivers, 115, 185

Uber, 70, 75, 76, 78, 82
undercommons, 174
Underground Railroad: solidarity
    of, 23–24, 58–59, *59*; space for,
    59
unionized worker cooperatives,
    78; in Britain, 81; in France, 74;
    in Italy, 74
Union Square Park, *3*
United States: capitalism in, 53;
    caregivers in, 160; caregiving
    crisis in, 113–123, 185; cartel law
    in, 77; cooperatives in, 74, 76,
    77; domestic workers in, 5, 171;
    feminism in, 35; housekeepers
    in, 160; housing shortage in,
    185; nannies in, 160; nuclear
    family in, 154n1; ownership in,
    154n3; platform cooperatives
    in, 83; private property in,
    128; town halls in, 1; transition
    design in, 53–55. *See also*
    specific locations and topics
Up-and-Go, 75
U.S. Digital Response, 95–96
user engagement, in new
    collectives, 135–136

Valery, Ernst, 64, 187, 188
venture capital model, 72;
    cooperatives and, 79; in
    Germany, 77
Villas de San Pablo. *See* Quipu
voice-over-internet-protocol
    (VOIP), 166
Voices from the CareForce, 173
VOIP. *See* voice-over-internet-
    protocol
Voz Mob, 166

Wang, Tricia, 88–97
Willis, Anne-Marie, 51
Wodiczko, Krzysztof, 171
women: in cooperatives, 64,
    73–74; as domestic workers,
    165–166; immigrant women of
    color, 5; monuments to, 4.
women of color: caregiving by,
    17, 27n19; in gig economy
    cooperatives, 79; immigrants, 5

Young, Barbara, 25n3
Yung, Raylene, 95–96
Yusoff, Kathryn, 27n19, 177

Zapatista movement, of Mexico,
    46–47
Zhang, Daya, *142*
zoning envelopes, 4

Printed and bound by CPI Group (UK) Ltd, Croydon, CR0 4YY

15/01/2024

08222306-0001